From Origin to Ecology

From Origin to Ecology

Nature and the Poetry of W. S. Merwin

Jane Frazier

Madison • Teaneck
Fairleigh Dickinson University Press
London: Associated University Presses

© 1999 by Associated University Presses, Inc.

Associated University Presses
440 Forsgate Drive
Cranbury, NJ 08512

Associated University Presses
16 Barter Street
London WC1A 2AH, England

Associated University Presses
P.O. Box 338, Port Credit
Mississauga, Ontario
Canada L5G 4L8

The paper used in this publication meets the requirements of the American National Standard for Permanence of Paper for Printed Library Materials Z39.48–1984.

Library of Congress Cataloging-in-Publication Data

Frazier, Jane, 1959–
    From origin to ecology : nature and the poetry of W.S. Merwin / Jane Frazier.
        p.   cm.
    Includes bibliographical references and index.
    ISBN 0-8386-3799-X (alk. paper)
    1. Merwin, W. S. (William Stanley), 1927–   —Knowledge—Natural history.   2. American poetry—Themes, motives.   3. Ecology in literature.   4. Nature in literature.   I. Title.
    PS3563.E75Z67   1999
    811'.54—dc21
                                                                        98-54595
                                                                        CIP

PRINTED IN THE UNITED STATES OF AMERICA

As a blind man, lifting a curtain, knows it is morning,
I know this change:
On one side of silence there is no smile;
But when I breathe with the birds,
The spirit of wrath becomes the spirit of blessing,
And the dead begin from their dark to sing in my sleep.
—Theodore Roethke, "Journey to the Interior"

Contents

Acknowledgments

F OR THE PRODUCTION OF THIS BOOK, I WOULD LIKE TO FIRST ACKNOWLEDGE its early shapers: Michael Dean, Benjamin Franklin Fisher, David Galef, and Edward Sisson of the University of Mississippi. I would also like to thank Thomas Russell for inviting me to the University of Memphis and Martin Lammon, Robert Viau, and Pamela Nolte-Viau for inviting me to Georgia College and State University when Mr. Merwin was visiting. *South Dakota Review*, *Weber Studies*, and *Style* first published portions of the text and were instrumental in its development. My gratitude to Associated University Presses and to their patient editors. Finally, I would like to express my debt to the late Evans Harrington and to Colby Kullman for their tireless encouragement of my endeavors.

* * *

Bly, Robert. Excerpts from "Hunting Pheasants in a Cornfield," from *Silence in the Snowy Fields,* © 1962, Wesleyan University Press. Reprinted by permission of Robert Bly.

Dudley, Michael Kioni. Excerpts from *A Hawaiian Nation 1: Man, Gods, and Nature,* © 1990 are reprinted by permission of Michael Kioni Dudley.

Kumin, Maxine. Excerpts from "Noted in *The New York Times*," from *Nurture,* © 1989 are reprinted by permission of Maxine Kumin. Excerpts from "Repent," from *Selected Poems: 1960–1990,* © 1989 are reprinted by permission of W. W. Norton & Company.

Lieberman, Laurence. Excerpts from *"New Poetry: The Church of Ash"* by Laurence Lieberman from *The Yale Review,* © 1973 are reprinted by permission of *The Yale Review.*

From Origin to Ecology

Origin

As the earth and its life forms have evolved, so has the poetry of one of its singers. In the 1950s and early 1960s, when William Stanley Merwin was publishing his first books of poetry employing fixed forms and traditional devices, often dealing with classical subjects, and when he was publishing a rather straightforward free verse, there was little indication that his work would later diverge so radically in style or that his consciousness concerning one topic would develop to the point that he would become a leading figure on its behalf. Although Merwin's poetry is well known for its expression of alienation, over the years he has increasingly demonstrated a shift toward affirming humankind's place in the natural world, the necessity of reconceptualizing this relationship, and the human responsibilty for maintaining and supporting the ecosystem in which we exist. Now, near the close of the century and the millenium, his writings consistently vocalize the urgency of reestimations of our ideological models of nature and the need for commitment to measures that will promote the environmental integrity of the planet.

Merwin began his public career at age twenty-five by winning the Yale Series of Younger Poets' Award for 1952, giving him his first book, *A Mask for Janus*. Since that time, he has produced seventeen volumes of poetry, more than twenty translations, four books of prose, and a host of essays and reviews. The son of a Presbyterian minister, he was born in New York, was raised in New Jersey and Pennsylvania, and has lived in Majorca, Spain, England, France, New York, Mexico, and Hawaii. From the Pulitzer Prize to the Bollingen Prize, there is hardly an award for poetry that Merwin has not garnered. Often a contributor to such exclusive literary publications as *The New Yorker* and *The Paris Review*, he nevertheless has taken his appeals for environmental reformation to the pages of the more popular *Sierra* and *The New York Times Magazine*. Recently, he has initiated the reprinting of and written an introduction for *Last of the Curlews,* a novel on one level about the near extinction of a bird known as the Eskimo curlew, but on another about the potential extinction of any species. These ecocommunal concerns reflect a dramatic transformation in a poet who first expressed a tense, uneasy sense of natural belonging and whose portrayals of earthly absences became a typical subject in his work.

By taking a glimpse at his personal life, we find that Merwin's environmentalism does not simply reside in his writings and statements. For the past two decades he has lived in a rather remote area on the northeast coast of Maui, where he and his wife, Paula, have been working to reforest eighteen acres of land ruined by pineapple farming fifty years ago. The grounds have been replanted with lush, diverse vegetation, including koa, mango, banana, and palm trees, as well as hibiscus and gardenia plants, heliconias, birds-of-paradise, and ferns of various types. The species are indigenous to Hawaii, and part of the purpose of the garden is to cultivate endangered native plants. Through this labor, Merwin is able to combine his love for gardening with the needs of his immediate environment, and, as he has stated, the issues remain "intimate" and "familiar."[1]

Like the flowering of his garden, Merwin's poetry similarly flowered in multiple ways after his re-creation of style. I propose that Merwin's shift to the broken syntax and stanzas of *The Moving Target* (1963) precipitated in him a liberation not only stylistic but philosophical as well. Not insignificantly, 1963 is also the year in which he moved to a farm in rural France where he stayed for several years, having been disturbed for some time by the accelerating devastation to the ecosystem and, in his view, the related military aggression exemplified by Vietnam and the Cuban missile crisis. It was after his stylistic change that the poetry began to take chances by experimenting with modes of representation and modes of conceptualizing that had been largely unseen in this nevertheless most precocious of poets. Although Merwin had always exhibited a penchant for wryly uncovering human blindnesses, with the explosive new style a concomitant free play with perceptual boundaries became manifest. In this first book to employ his new deconstructed style, and with this open, unrestricted form, the poetry welcomed the surreal and mysterious, a necessary position for a poet seeking clues to the enigma of human existence. With the removal of many of the stylistic strictures of his first four books and the expanding of his subject matter, Merwin has been much more free to experiment with ways of producing a poetry that seeks a greater understanding of living relationships. As a result and as a reason for this move to freer form, Merwin has discovered a poetic place for himself—the wandering, alienated poet of the modern age has found a "home" within the ecosystem and a tangible entity whose cause he can espouse for global betterment. His "other" career, only superficially distinct from that of his writing, has been that of a translator of poetry from Persius to Osip Mandelstam. As a result of this work, we see in Merwin's own poetry traces of the vibrant imagism of Pablo Neruda, the aphorism of Antonio Porchia, and the holistic reverence of the Quechua.

The tradition of nature writing is long and varied, and, like any good poet, Merwin establishes his own ideas on the topic. From this tradition, however, it is evident that certain concepts that appear in Henry David Thoreau are also present in Merwin. Thoreau, by Merwin's own accounts, serves as the writer of nature for whom he claims to have the greatest admiration. Thoreau's intimate observations of the living world and his humility in the face of it in *Walden* and other works correspond to Merwin's approach quite strikingly. Although Thoreau delivers un-Merwin-like transcendental statements and although ethical messages concerning the human community are often woven throughout his writings, I propose that the living world survives as a subject in itself, that it often does not become subsumed by an overweening ideological agenda, however much ideology may course through his writing. It also appears to me fruitless to try to draw too many fine lines between politics and earth, because the economies of nature he records are offered for their own sake as well as for what they may bequeath to humankind as worthy example. When, for instance, Thoreau records the frugality of nature, he offers an ecological and not just an economical or moral lesson for humankind.

Within the works of Thoreau, from *A Week on the Concord and Merrimack Rivers* to his final essays, such modern concerns as how humankind is to imagine and treat the ecosystem, and, not insignificantly, how it treats us, are omnipresent. Many of his pages brim with precise description of such phenomena as rivers, mountains, moose, and beach grass. Thoreau takes great pains to depict how people in various localities interact with their environs, some wisely, some not, and his prose details a varied and magnificent planet. Even within Thoreau, we discover the necessity of tough-minded observation. If he had never presented the awful aspects of the natural world, as the ferocity of the rapids in *The Maine Woods* or the dangerous ocean in *Cape Cod*, we would have to doubt the accuracy of his reflections. Nature is both magnanimous and threatening, and few writers have examined it with such a careful eye or have demonstrated that they have learned so much in the process.

Some recent criticism on Thoreau has theorized that his philosophy was not stagnant, that it was visibly in a state of ongoing development and, as such, often reveals conflicting viewpoints. This thesis may help to explain the attractiveness of Thoreau to Merwin. As a writer who has undergone his own significant alterations of consciousness, the exploratory, evolving aspect of Thoreau's writings may have provided a personal reference point. At times, Thoreau may smother natural observation in search of Emersonian "correspondences" to the human imagination, and there is no escaping his fame as a representative of the transcendental movement, but his sincere environmentalism consistently sounds in his work. His sketches of the writer in the process of discovering nature have no doubt fostered in the later poet an affinity for his precursor's work. It also hardly needs mention that at the time Thoreau was composing his essays, protection of the environment was practically unheard of in light of the popular belief in the boundlessness of nature.

Like Thoreau, what Merwin strives for in many of his nature poems is contact with a lost, original world, free from the ontologically insular and physically threatening forces of industrialization and technology—a condition in which humans exist in community with their surroundings. Merwin's other major approach to nature is to lament its disappearance in the modern age, a theme that finds expression in his poetry of humans' division from nature and our outright destruction of it.

The poetry that focuses on the original world, which I shall simply call the "origin," seeks a timeless existence in which humans are participants rather than rulers; or, in this project, the biocentric rather than the homocentric constitutes the object of literary desire. In the literature of the Western world, we may trace the concept of origin back at least as far as the book of Genesis with its Garden of Eden and to Hesiod's *Works and Days*, which speaks of the parallel Golden Age of Greece. In the poems of origin, Merwin seeks to do away with the logical categories with which we perceive and order the world and turns instead to a mysterious, primal experience. What keeps Merwin from being mystical in the fashion of the British Romantics, however, is that nature is not "transcended"; its value is inherent. In this poststructuralist age of what Lawrence Buell cites as the "hermeneutics of skepticism," my identification of a mythical strain in Merwin runs the risk of exiling his lyrics into the Siberian landscape of male-dominated, idyllic-settler writing.[2] However, I believe that much of Merwin's poetry situates the poet one-on-one with the planet and that his long-standing expression of disdain for Euro-American antagonism to the landscape and its indigenous peoples should remove any suspicion of Merwin secretly representing a culture of domination or even complacent acquiescence to the status quo. One may be tempted to ignore mythic elements in favor of a selective political reading. Yet, in Merwin, representations of nature resonate with idyllic overtones (though sometimes muted) often enough that my reading of his nature poetry cannot dispense with them. What is essential in appraising his poetry is that Eden has never been envisioned in the American enterprise but only in nature itself.

In a balanced definition of American pastoral, Buell claims that the genre may not be confined to a "single ideological position"—of hegemonic conservatism or of undifferentiated anticonsensualism.[3] For Buell, the question of the dichotomy in naturism of "the centripetal pull of consensualism that threatens to draw the radical text over into the sleepy safe domain of nature's nationism, the ho-hum pieties of American civil religion," and "the centifugal impulse always incipient, though usually contained within modest limits, for pastoral to form itself in opposition to social institutions" must be recognized.[4] Wendell Berry's agrarianism, he notes, for example, embraces an ideological stance distinct from that of Thomas Jefferson; Rachel Carson's *Silent Spring* includes a pastoral passage that far from legitimizes her contemporary milieu; Thoreau's move to Walden is both a rejection of mainstream values and a reenactment of pioneer history.[5] Ultimately, Buell's argument, which further exposes the imperialistic motivations of European pastoral literature situated in "new worlds," concludes that, with all of its shortcomings, the pastoral is an ideologically sound mode of representation for its referential and experiential character, which may foster ecological consciousness. Naturism is simply too large a category, containing too many conflicting or disparate concepts, to dismiss as hegemonic.

My reading of Merwin is, admittedly, even more supportive of his work than Buell's is of Thoreau's. I propose that Merwin's representations of the natural world—even those that to some critics have appeared to abstract or even allegorize it—are part and parcel of an environmentalism that is not apolitical. A poem that ostensibly appears to be a contemplation—even a mythopoeic musing—upon a valley scene merely manifests a facet of the imagination that is working, however subtly, to efface the homocentric position. There are a few instances in Merwin's poetry where he has questionably employed anthropomorphization in relation to animals, but I argue that his work overall demonstrates a mind moving toward a natural understanding reflective of current ecological thinking rather than the philosophies of the past.

At this point we should take a close look at the term *nature* as we shall use it. Gary Snyder, a contemporary of Merwin, explains that the word derives from the Latin *natura*, which means "birth, constitution, character, course of things." Snyder explains that the word has come to have two different meanings, one that is approximated by the outdoors and all living things, and the other that includes this realm as well as all of the "products of human action and intention." The second definition would not exclude anything in our universe as "unnatural," not cities nor the waste products of factories.[6] The nature that I would like to consider is of the first variety—the phenomena not created by humans yet including human behaviors and ways of living in accord with original phenomena. For clarity, Snyder prefers to use the term *wilderness* instead. He points out that wilderness has been typically explained in negatives—wild things have been seen as "unruly," "uncultivated," and "rude." From another point of view, however, "wild" may mean "free," "self-maintaining," and "independent."[7] For Snyder and for Merwin, the cultivated is valid only when it is in harmony with the surrounding wild environment. As Snyder puts it, "This is acknowledging that the source of fertility ultimately is the 'wild.'"[8] We learn from both poets that nature by word and by deed has long been pushed away from much of human society in order that society may imagine itself as different from it. To poets like Merwin and Snyder, nothing could be more self-deluding, and nothing could be more destructive. Thus, we have the return to origin attempted by Merwin and by many throughout literary history.

A sampling of lines from volumes beginning with *The Carrier of Ladders* exhibits a plenitude that is present in the earth and that has its implications for us: "I must be led by what was given to me / as streams are led by it"; "this morning the light will speak to me / of what concerns me"; "the sun as it sets through the forest of windows /

unrolls slowly its / unrepeatable secret."[9] Faith in nature grows slowly for Merwin, a poet who is known by many for his dark brooding over the sins of humankind and the alienation of living in the world—even the natural world. Conflicting ideas over nature's restorative powers may even be found within the same volume, but Merwin's trust in the earth increases steadily over time, and it is this impulse that, I believe, controls his poetry by the late 1970s.

One of Merwin's prose poems, "A Conversation," from *Houses and Travellers*, works as an excellent gloss to his ideas about origin in the lyrical poems. "A Conversation" depicts a dialogue going on within nature, in this case between two different types of landscape, a garden and a desert. The narrator says that he can hear the discussion between the garden and the desert when the wind shifts direction, and that what he hears is the two of them discussing their dreams together. The relationship between these two parts of the earth is presented as symbiotic—on an imaginative level they need each other, and through this scenario the poet is able to convey his belief in the interrelatedness of parts of the planet:

> They tell their dreams to each other, the garden and the desert. They dream above all of each other. The desert dreams of the garden inside it. It loves the garden. It embraces the garden. It wants to turn it into desert. The garden lives within itself. It dreams of the desert all around it, and of its difference from the desert, which it knows is as frail as feeling.[10]

Although they are two different types of terrain, and although one wishes similarity between the two while the other relishes their differences, their dissimilarities both physical and philosophical actually seem to support their relationship. Their symbiosis is evidenced by their conversation, as, biologically, nature functions in dialogue.

The narrator recognizes his ability to hear the garden and the desert, which may have preceded his awareness and anyone else's. He realizes an original connection between humans and nature engrained in the individual psyche:

> It must have been a long time since I first heard them talking. I must have heard them when I was two. I must have heard them when I was one, and so on. Perhaps before I was born. Or anyone was born. Or any roundness became an egg. Or the water was born, cooling on a high rock, prophesying tears, prophesying eyes.[11]

This cognitive bond is echoed often throughout Merwin's canon and often more directly. As a somewhat more earthly cousin to the Platonic notion of recollection of the "forms" where people have an inborn sense of certain concepts, this type of knowledge comes to narrators from the ancient past, from a past that precedes history and perhaps humankind. John Keats and William Wordsworth also refer to recollections of nature in their poetry; *Endymion* asserts, "Nor do we merely feel these essences / For one short hour; ... They alway must be with us, or we die."[12] It is Merwin, however, who takes remembrance into the original—the personal opens out toward the species and all species. In one stanza of "Looking for Mushrooms at Sunrise," the deliverance of primal memory to the present in a specific locus prompts resonance of an alternate consciousness: "Where they appear it seems I have been before / I recognize their haunts as though remembering / Another life."[13]

The prescription for humankind is an openness to listen to what nature is saying. Like the world, which has wanted to speak from the beginning, "light" in "A Conversation" has had "the colors hidden inside it," and, implicitly, this beauty can be seen with the right vision.[14] Merwin also uses light, one of his most basic elements in the universe, to represent that which contains the knowledge of the whole: "forgetting nothing from the beginning, prophesying the end of knowledge, prophesying the wilderness, prophesying the garden, prophesying the wilderness dreaming that it was a garden."[15] The poem espouses a philosophy and common sense: various aspects of the world do not exist independently of one another, and knowledge is not the domain of humans, but something we are partakers of. Thoreau tells us that he went to the woods to "see if I could not learn what it had to teach, and not, when I came to die, discover that I had not lived."[16] Merwin as well has faith in the integral character of the world, and often mourns humankind's separation from this order, sometimes in the form of quiet elegy, sometimes with unapologetic jeremiad.

Whereas the dialogue of "A Conversation" reflects the basic law of ecology—the biosphere's interactiveness—the simple fact that "A Conversation" is a poem mirrors nature analogically in the view of William Rueckert. Rueckert proposes that poems may be seen as green plants: they assist in establishing creativity and community, and when their stored energy is released to others, matter (consciousness) is raised from a lower to a higher order. The poem, like the green plant, traps energy on its road to dispersal and loss (entropy) by what

Ian McHarg has labeled "negentropy."[17] Furthermore, in dissemination through reading, teaching, and critical discourse, the stored energy of the poem flows outward into a symbiotic relationship with the reader. In the classroom, the creation of community by the discussion of a poem may be quite noticeable.[18] Thus, Merwin's poetry situates him, metaphorically, into an ecological role. The difficulty with the application of Rueckert's thesis to Merwin is that, typically, on an experiential level nature is approached by the poet/narrator in a condition of solitude; and, sometimes, Merwin's antihumanism nears that of a Robinson Jeffers. How can a poet who scorns humanity fit into the communal scheme? Or, in challenge to Rueckert, why would a true naturist be concerned with the dissemination of a poem? It appears that Merwin's basic relationship to the human community is that of ecoprophet, and as the speaker perennially returning from the wilderness, he demonstrates a tacit concern for humanity and the rest of the world in his warnings. True, the hard-edged 1967 volume *The Lice* contains militant expressions of antihumanism; yet these are short-lived in terms of his career, and concern for the inclusive planet, humans and all, I argue directs his later writings.

The Compass Flower, published in 1977, demonstrates the certainty of a perceivable "spiritual" wealth within the natural world by this point in his career. Apart from a series of city poems that it contains, the volume largely reflects a pastoral atmosphere—and the pastoral is sometimes taken into the primal. From *The Compass Flower*, "Summer Night on the Stone Barrens" focuses upon origin and its imaginative impact upon a speaker. The speaker witnesses an initial moment of emergence in a setting where nature has the singular voice: "In the first hours of darkness / while the wide stones are still warm from the sun / through the hush waiting for thunder / a body falls out of a tree / rat or other soft skin."[19] The narrator hears and sees different elements as they make themselves evident in the night—lightning, crickets, owls, the moon—and with these he is led to ponder the creators of the world, whoever or whatever they were: "I am under the ancient roof alone / the beams are held up by forgotten builders / of whom there were never pictures."[20] The unknown shapers of the universe are equated with the language we do not know of them; they are "voices not heard," which gives them the power of a legacy not revealed by speech and writing but rather by the architecture that they have left behind.[21]

To the unheard voices, the narrator expresses a relationship he cannot quite control. From some, he says he moves away, but some draw him toward an insight into the universe: "the stillness is a black pearl / and I can see into it while the animals fall / one at a time at immeasurable intervals."[22] We should observe that this understanding comes in a moment of "stillness," a recurring concept in Merwin. The chaos of the modern world is excluded as the narrator learns within the context of a primal garden with its animals falling in a place seemingly outside of time. Out of language, out of time, out of civilization, the stone barrens is the archetypal setting for the return to the original world; it is an Eliadean "sacred space" that Merwin goes so far as to describe here, at least within the imagination of the narrator. Keats's opening lines in *Endymion*, "A thing of beauty is a joy for ever: / Its loveliness increases; it will never / Pass into nothingness; but still will keep / A bower quiet for us, and a sleep / Full of sweet dreams, . . ." praise a garden also enduring and benificent, although more idealized, or cultivated.[23] Beauty in Keats's poem even protects the garden, as all sacred spaces are protected. Merwin's ancient world also comprises truth, beauty, and knowledge but only implicitly, in the descriptions of images and the musings of speakers. "Summer Night on the Stone Barrens" offers as much of origin as is available; it remains just outside of the narrator's grasp. Yet how is the move made now from origins to earthly? How can the romanticized ideal relate to a factual, gritty, present-day planet?

Although origin is a move back toward first connections, or, in a sense, a regression, it is, in a second sense, a "beginning" for Merwin as a poet. Origin establishes a starting point for his narrators in situating themselves in the context of the earth; I intend this historically as well as in relation to the individual poem, because the concept appears much more in the books of the seventies than in later volumes. Later revisits to the ideal appear, but this common topic is primarily evident in the decade following *The Lice*. Although it may cloak itself as merely a poetic dead end, a rarefied never-attainable garden, this first world initiates a type of process in the poetry; even in its unattainability a heightened understanding of earthly relationships is produced. The contemplation of the green idyllic for any writer may lay the ground for the cultivation of the ecological mind-set. Once the poet estab-lishes that nature is the object of desire, the epistemological shift to a more realistic representation of ecological relationships may follow if the poet does not become lost in the never-never land of his own signifiers, and, I will argue, this shift does follow in the case of Merwin.

The importance of the imagination when we speak of the origin in Merwin can hardly be stressed enough. The imagination's active role, as inaugurator and contributor to original understanding, is emphasized in "Fishing," also from *The Compass Flower*. Here, the narrator relates the moment of connection to an earlier world as having happened in his childhood while waiting for a fish to strike. Whereas fishing is often perceived as a simple pastime of youth, the ramifications of this experience are much more far-reaching:

> moment of fire
> above a drum of white
> stone water
> with the line vibrating through it
> one-string harp
> never to be out of the feeling in my fingers
> name from before anyone was born
> bright color in darkness through half a life
> beating suddenly toward me[24]

With the words "feeling," "vibrating," and "beating," Merwin incorporates the language of the sensual; yet, mystery and, more importantly, consciousness take precedence. In Orphic tradition, the fishing line, a "one-string harp," plays the "name from before anyone was born" of the source that the speaker dreams of meeting. In the scheme of evolution, the hidden fish brings to mind the watery ancestors of all life. However, whether the narrator as a child comprehends classical or evolutionary connections is unimportant. What he does sense is an ancient relationship to the source and kinship to the fish as a living being. That the power of origin has an unknown name, that it is a "bright color in darkness," underscores its enigma and its value; origin is established as a benificent well from which humans may draw. The narrator understands, furthermore, that he will never "be out of the feeling," that the source will remain available to him for the rest of his life. It is primal and strange, and it is nevertheless the return to lost familial relationships.

When revelation, or contact with origin, does occur, it is in an instant, but the narrators have also psychologically worked up to that point. The moment of recognition is the culmination of a process that the poem has led us through; in fact, the speakers' delineated thought processes are the active and evolving consciousness of the poems. Although not psychological portraits, these poems usually portray the thinking of the narrators as they experience something for the first time, which, paradoxically, is removed from time. In "Fishing," the name comes to him "through half a life" and is "from before anyone was born"—it evinces the same timelessness as the milieu of "Summer Night on the Stone Barrens."

In "A Contemporary," from the same volume, the narrator, wishing to join the unified earth, uses the language of time—"day and night"—to indicate how he will free himself of it: "I would be green with white roots / feel worms touch my feet as a bounty / have no name and no fear / turn naturally to the light / know how to spend the day and night / climbing out of myself / all my life."[25] His wish to "[climb] out of [himself]" and to have "no name and no fear" furthermore tells us something of the dispensing of the human, or disembodiment, that is so often found in these poems. In this case, the speaker goes so far as to wish himself a part of the vegetable kingdom in a state of eternal (or at least lifelong) growth. His "greening" is conceptual, but his underlying desire and its alterations of consciousness are quite real.

Glen A. Love asserts that a redefinition of "pastoral" that is appropriate for the future requires experience with the living world to be established as something more than a temporary "excursion." The "pastoral" for now and for the future demands a better science of nature, an improved understanding of the natural world's complexities and energies, and a deeper analysis of human priorities.[26] For Merwin's "pastoral" to be valid, then, it must signify something more than a weekend retreat. When we look at the canon of Merwin for evidence of where his naturism has taken him, poetry and prose on the historical and current ecological condition of real species and communities of species are plentiful. It seems that, for this poet, the poetry of origin, the pull toward beginnings, facilitates a recognition of the earth profoundly related to environmental cognizance and self-examination. Even disembodiment, a technique we shall examine later, has as its ultimate goal something very concrete: a valid bond with the planet that will determine action and consciousness.

Ed Folsom believes that Thoreau's reverence for the living world and keen insight into and attachment to the places he lives in relates to Merwin beginning with *The Compass Flower* and going through *Finding the Islands* and *Opening the Hand*, the last of Merwin's volumes written at the time of Folsom's essay.[27] Whereas Merwin's role of partaker in the natural world is evident in these three volumes, I propose that it did not begin there. *The Carrier of Ladders* (1970) and *Writings to an Unfinished Accompaniment* (1973) also strongly express the desire for a connection with the planet, although their poems are not generally as celebratory. We even see scattered evidence of this attitude in such works as "Lemuel's Blessing" and "Daybreak" in the 1963 volume, *The Moving Target.* The same young poet who wrote such spare, gloomy poetry about existence, political corruption, and our reckless treatment of the natural world also found voice to reflect upon the bounty of the planet. As Folsom observes, Thoreau often informs what have seemed to many readers of Merwin the strange pastoral moments that have been a part of this poet's work even at his most pessimistic points.[28]

When asked in an interview with Ed Folsom and Cary Nelson why he was attracted to Thoreau and not to Walt Whitman, Merwin stressed Thoreau's identification with nature, his conceptual oneness with it:

> I suppose the way in which he meant "In wildness is the preservation of the world" for one thing. Or the recognition that the human cannot exist independently in a natural void; whatever the alienation is that we feel from the natural world, we are not in fact alienated, so we cannot base our self-righteousness on that difference. We're part of the whole thing. And the way Thoreau, very differently from Whitman, even in a paragraph takes his own perception and develops it into a deeper and deeper way of seeing something—the actual seeing in Thoreau is one of the things that draws me to him. I think that Thoreau saw in a way that nobody had quite seen before; it was American in that sense. . . . Indeed I've suspected for a long time that an American poet's sympathy would tend to go either toward Whitman or toward Thoreau, not toward both. . . . And for Thoreau, when he sees it [the natural world], it's alive, completely alive, not a detail in a piece of rhetoric. And he leaves open what its significance is. He realizes that the intensity with which he's able to see it is its significance. This is an immense gesture of wisdom in Thoreau that I miss in Whitman.[29]

Thoreau for Merwin represents the writer willing to allow himself to become personally absorbed in the natural world, to muse upon it and learn ways of living from it. To Merwin, Whitman's admiration of nature seems to include it only as an extension of the self, and his sympathy for earth merely replicates his sympathy for everything else, including factories, railroads, and cities. Merwin's reading of the *Leaves of Grass* poet does appear unduly harsh, yet understandable in light of the national expansionism justified and lauded by Whitman and Merwin's near-nausea at our New World history. His critique is further aesthetically explainable when we consider Whitman's bold, egoistic voice booming from page to page, in sharp contradistinction to the spare, reticent, and sometimes coy lines of the later poet. As Merwin states in the Nelson and Folsom interview, the intensity with which Thoreau views nature indicates his conviction of its value. For Merwin and for Thoreau, the living world is something that they turn to with passion; it cannot be severed from their philosophy without detroying it. To follow out Merwin's argument, with Whitman it may be possible to exclude nature from his list of items admired, and he would still find other things to celebrate, because the celebratory mode and the self, turning restlessly from item to item, and not the "thing" itself—nature—is his real work.

Repeatedly in *Walden*, Thoreau gives us passages of contemplation of the world and its application to his own actions and epistemology. Once in a while, he will explain what the awareness of the earth can mean to the human, as he does in one segment from *Walden:*

> And we are enabled to apprehend at all what is sublime and noble only by the perpetual instilling and drenching of the reality that surrounds us. The universe constantly and obediently answers to our conceptions; whether we travel fast or slow, the track is laid for us. Let us spend our lives in conceiving then. The poet or the artist never had yet so fair and noble a design but some of his posterity at least could accomplish it.[30]

Thoreau's homily implies that, from the example that nature gives us of simplifying, we, too, can cut ourselves loose from the frivolities of living and thus concentrate upon immediate wonders. Thoreau's formula has more of the artist's shaping, the "conceiving," in it than Merwin's, yet it still emphasizes "instilling" the world into our psychic veins. Though a concept much expressed in Romantic literature, the tenet of the absorption of the earthly into the self must also occur in any modern-day poetics of nature. Otherwise, the psyche is relegated to a removed contemplation of the world that might as well take place in a condition of virtual reality.

The awakening or conversion theme that Thoreau avidly repeats occurs in Merwin's "The New Season," from *Opening the Hand*, and in "September Plowing," from *The Compass Flower*. In these poems, specific elements are depicted as sentient and able to bestow meaning in a manner that returns in a few apocalyptic poems in *The Rain in the Trees*. In "The New Season," all of nature becomes conscious and vocal, whereas in "September Plowing," beings driven by original memory parallel this process happening in the narrator. "The New Season" opens with the narrator of the poem going outside of his house with his dog on the third night of autumn to scare away some rats that he has heard, but the true source of the noise becomes uncertain. From an everyday event, such as checking around a house, the poem then moves to a numinous awareness of elements and creatures: "worms are awake under the leaves / beetles are awake eating / upside down in the dark / leaves are awake hearing / in the complete night."[31] The "leaves" become tropes for all of the world; all of nature is cognizant. The night is "complete" like the natural world itself and requires humans to symbolically step out of their constructions. The poet walks into a sentient community of nonhuman life, which makes human life in comparison seem stifled and isolated.

"September Plowing" adds the component of prelapsarian memory to consciousness with creatures who are tied to nature by their memories of the seasons just as humans are—"the hare keeps looking up remembering."[32] Even the "dark oak woods" that "leap up and shine" play an active role.[33] That animals and traditionally unconscious elements in Western thought—such as trees, wind, and water—are imbued with not only understanding but wisdom is not unusual in Merwin. From this viewpoint, revival for earth and human may be quite explicit: "oh it is the autumn light // that brings everything back in one hand / the light again of beginnings / the amber appearing as amber."[34] Otherwise, we may be left as the narrator of "The New Season" and his dog, waiting on the verge, the edge that is more typical: "I stand with a flashlight / in a smell of fruit / and we wait."[35]

When engaged, recollection puts the events of the present into a far-reaching chain of similar moments. Charles Altieri observes that memory is essential to the grasping of greater truths in Merwin because it acts as a device where the normally restricted self and the contingent present are allowed to join in a larger "transpersonal" union.[36] As Altieri notes, too, Merwin's discussion of the poetry of Jean Follain offers an excellent sketch of his own view of memory:

Memory, as distinct from the past it draws on, is what makes the past a key to the mystery that stays with us and does not change: the present. . . .

Follain's concern is finally with the mystery of the present—the mystery which gives the recalled concrete details their form, at once luminous and removed, when they are seen at last in their places, as they seem to be in the best of his poems. This is their value "in themselves." At the same time it is what gives them the authority of parts of a rite, of an unchanging ceremony heralding some inexorable splendor, over a ground of silence. And for Follain it is a fulfillment not only of a need for ceremony but of a fondness for the ceremonious, in which each detail, seen as itself, is an evocation of the processions of an immeasurable continuum.[37]

Earlier in this discussion of Follain, Merwin speaks of the "'impersonal,' receptive, but essentially unchanging gaze" that stands in the place of the first person in Follain's work.[38] Merwin's own impersonal, or disembodied, speakers come to us with little detail and act as the receptors of the particular present that has its own value and its value in a "continuum" of such occurrences. The significance of the particulars as they appear at the moment is not negated; on the contrary, they are as sharp as ever. However, by seeing them as part of a pattern of such recurring events, they are more acutely appreciable. T. S. Eliot's famous passage in "Tradition and the Individual Talent" reiterates the concept by placing the timeless and temporal, both separately and simultaneously, within the context of literary memory. This, to Eliot, constitutes the ideal historical or traditional sense.

As in the incantatory final passage of *The Waste Land* and as in Follain, the importance of events in Merwin occurs when they are presented as the parts of a "rite." The religious modeling of Merwin's poetry of origin, the attempt to reach origin through spare, prayerlike poetry, also heralds the "splendor over a ground of silence." In one poem from *Opening the Hand*, "The Middle of Summer," the subject who is addressed has learned to tap into the reservoir of memory that embraces the timeless flow: "By now you have envisaged / in lives as many as those / of a tree in spring / the summer nights / in the cabin by the lake / with the sun never setting."[39] Nature is replete with flux: birth, growth, death, decay. Yet, it is these components of existence that create patterns. Origin places the real, tangible things of the world into patterns that illuminate their value through the lens of regeneration. Consequently, value exists for the human in seeing oneself as part of the continuum. The subject of "The Middle of Summer" perceives himself as a "shadow" on the water, not obscured, but rather reflected as a being, a part of the earthly march:

"and your long shadow walking / on the still water // that is what you go on seeing / at that latitude / as the water turns silent and then / begins to tremble."[40]

The rites and patterns of the origin poems are analogous to those of religion, to those that would be typically termed "mystical," but in Merwin the mystery is confined to the wonder of the repetition of events and our interaction with them, rather than to the presence of an otherworldly force. If there is any outside "mystical" force in Merwin, it is the force of earth itself within which these events take place.

Such reenactments in a real sense redeliver the timeless flow. Moving backward along time lines, we are released from temporal isolationism by the elements of origin. The transformational figure in "Under Black Leaves," from *Writings to an Unfinished Accompaniment*, is the cricket, whose auspicious ancestry lies in the cosmos, according to the poem's creation story. Here, creation and living beings are associated with the moon, stars, and geographic directions through relationships once recognized by our earliest ancestors. The moon was commonly related by early peoples to birth and death because it, visually, dies and is reborn regularly. The stars mapped out the skies for them, and the migrations of animals established geographic directions that they could follow: "old moon swollen with our shadow / bringing it / to birth one more time // ... one of the stars that does not know it is the south / the birds' way."[41] The poem then abruptly shifts to the narrator's release from that which is confining him to the present and the anthropocentric, though we may find Merwin's employment of surrealistic metaphors to accomplish his effect obtuse: "the mouse is no longer afraid of me / the moth ... has been taken away ... nails have been drawn out of my ears."[42] Importantly, the events of the present fuse with a creation story that we are left with in small reminders:

certain stars leaving their doorways
hoped to become crickets
those soon to fall even threw
dice for the months
remembering some promise

that game was long before men
but the sounds travelled slowly
only now a few

arrive in the black trees
on the first night of autumn[43]

Significantly, the stars are the ones that remember "some promise" and come into the world as crickets, again imparting a "consciousness" to the universe and an interrelatedness among its parts.

Mark Christhilf believes that "Under Black Leaves" is based upon an ancient Asian myth in which heaven and earth existed alongside one another, before the Fall. This creation myth depicts heaven and earth as closely resembling one another until the split, which leaves communication open afterward only through certain avenues, such as mountains and trees. Too, Christhilf points out that there are similar tales among the American Indians that Merwin was studying and translating at the time of the poem's composition.[44] Original closeness in Merwin between humans and nature parallels the closeness between earth and heaven in the story Christhilf cites. For both, division—or the Fall—has disrupted early unity and perfect communication.

On the one hand, that we are left only with a legacy of the crickets in the trees that were once stars is the modern story—origin cannot be fully reexperienced. On the other hand, the arrival of the crickets each autumn is a sort of creation in itself—it is both a renewal and a reminder of the first creation. The origin story may be literally unrepeatable but may be typologically represented, as the creatures of the earth continue to regenerate, and as long as genesis remains engrained in the memories of the species of the planet. In "Birds at Noon" from *Houses and Travellers,* a speaker, in full awareness of his historiocultural distance from the original world, shifts from division to unity as he identifies with a jay flying through the woods and uttering the prophetic message: *"Change! Change!"*[45] Surrealism may work to the advantage of this prose poem, permitting the nearly magical chain of events as the other birds of the forest chime in chorus and "light up" the setting with the knowledge that they utter. Nature seems to have "spoken" to this narrator, and he is content with his newfound knowledge and his old loss: "When the singing stops I go on sitting with all that I remember, from there and from many distances, and with all that I have forgotten, in that grassy place in late Spring, after hearing something I wanted to know."[46] Unfortunately, there are many moments in Merwin where division overrides any possibility of recollection; the idyllic is often squashed by anthropocentric self-trust in ingenuity.

One *Walden* chapter, "The Bean-Field," offers a discussion on the primitive and a following valorization over civilized states, which, like the motif of recollection, is hardly new to romantic literature, especially the pastoral. Indian artifacts Thoreau uncovers while working the soil bring him to a meditation on early peoples and a joyful awareness of his surroundings:

> As I drew a still fresher soil about the rows with my hoe, I disturbed the ashes of unchronicled nations who in primeval years lived under these heavens, and their small implements of war and hunting were brought to the light of this modern day. They lay mingled with other natural stones, some of which bore the marks of having been burned by Indian fires, and some by the sun, and also bits of pottery and glass brought hither by the recent cultivators of the soil. When my hoe tinkled against the stones, that music echoed to the woods and the sky, and was an accompaniment to my labor which yielded an instant and immeasurable crop. It was no longer beans that I hoed, nor that I hoed beans; and I remembered with as much pity as pride, if I remembered at all, my acquaintances who had gone to the city to attend the oratorios.[47]

Notice, too, the epistemological distance between the narrator and his society. As the solitary receptor of the experience, he alone understands the profundity of the place in the moment, contemplating lost empires. For both writers this position creates something of a problem of isolationism and, perhaps, arrogance. However, I will contend, as earlier, that the solitary poet in the woods is part of the endeavor on the empirical level. The socialization of the project enters with the writing and dissemination of ideas, which, most assuredly, reveal conversionist ambitions. Yet, for some readers of Thoreau and Merwin, this posture never appears to overcome isolationism, and the reproach of the mass of humanity that sometimes occurs in both is too much to brook.

A few pages later, Thoreau, a student of the classics (as Merwin also is), draws upon his knowledge of mythology and ancient poetry to illustrate the historical importance of humankind's connection to the earth:

> Ancient poetry and mythology suggest, at least, that husbandry was once a sacred art; but it is pursued with irreverent haste and heedlessness

by us, our object being to have large farms and large crops merely. We
have no festival, nor procession, nor ceremony, not excepting our Cattle-
shows and so-called Thanksgivings, by which the farmer expresses a sense
of the sacredness of his calling, or is reminded of its sacred origin. It is
the premium and the feast which tempt him. He sacrifices not to Ceres
and the Terrestrial Jove, but to the infernal Plutus rather.[48]

As a tiller of the soil himself, the gardener who takes care of a small
parcel of land, Thoreau looks back to the ancient husbandman. Merwin does not write of the early farmer; his sentiments generally lean
more toward the wild and uncultivated, but he does project what
humans' earlier states must have been like and how those states have
vanished. In his two volumes of selected translations from the poetry
of other countries and ages, Merwin includes numerous poems from
American Indian cultures, ranging from Alaska to Peru. The inclusion
of these poems underscores his interest in ancient cultures where
the connection between the self and nature was given the highest
priority—the priority, as Thoreau notes, of being sacred. Gary Snyder
writes extensively in *The Practice of the Wild* of the meaning of the
living world in the cosmology of early humans. The worldwide, mystical human/nature bond began to disappear in the West with the
cutting of sacred groves by the Israelites, a practice that was later
continued by the Christians. Snyder explains: "It is only from very
old place-centered cultures that we hear of sacred groves, sacred land,
in a context of genuine belief and practice."[49] Some contemporary
Christian theologians, with Thomas Berry as the prime example,
believe that the West desperately needs a reevaluation of its attitudes
toward the natural world and that old dichotomies between nature
and God were never a healthy or moral way of perceiving the universe.
In Native American cultures, the universe was and is as much a part
of the conception of the self and the society as family or work roles.

The Indian translations of W. S. Merwin most commonly place
humans or animals in relation to the rest of the universe. Some speak
in ballad form of the original establishment of an order in creation;
some are a prayer to unnamed guiding forces in the universe; some
address an aspect of nature; and some are merely the lyrical musings
of an individual. "Prayer to the Corn in the Field," from Merwin's
second volume of selected translations, is a Tzeltal poem coming from
his experience of living in Chiapas in southern Mexico in the 1970s.
"Prayer to the Corn in the Field" describes the spiritual and factual

ties between nature and the Indian, the inextricable sense of his life in the life of all creation: "Sacred food / sacred bones // don't go to another house / don't go at all // ... if there are those of you / who were taken from your places // by the mountain lion / by the squirrel // ... come back along the trail / to our house."[50]

By praying to the corn, the speaker makes a prayer to the earth, asking that its nourishment not disappear to "another plant // another stone / another cave" and that it not escape because of the work of an animal.[51] Much more than a simple address to one source of food, this, as most of the Indian poems Merwin chooses, situates its subjects in the context of origin. The speaker's entire psychology, his ontological framework, depends upon the natural world and his place within it. The corn gives up its body so that others may be strengthened; the Native American prays and gives thanks because he sees the corn as a gift, to be used with humility and gratefulness.

On a few occasions, Merwin evokes the native consciousness he has translated. Employing the Indians' reverence for animals and their tales of animals' roles in the mystical and physical, Merwin's "The Black Jewel" offers us the primal through a cricket—the same vehicle in "Under Black Leaves." "The Black Jewel," from *Opening the Hand*, presents a narrator listening to the sounds of a cricket and all that surrounds it:

> In the dark
> there is only the sound of the cricket
>
> south wind in the leaves
> is the cricket
> so is the surf on the shore
> and the barking across the valley[52]

Deliberately or not, the poem follows an American Indian religious concept of the one as symbolic of the many. The cricket becomes the image of origin. Everything is contained in it, and everything has its basis in it. Like the elements and living things that the Indians look reverentially to, this creature is a part of diurnal life. The description of the cricket's voice as singular—"it has only the one sound"—may be deceptive on first glance.[53] As its being is universal, so is its voice, which initiates primal recollection in the narrator: "before I could talk / I heard the cricket / under the house / then I remembered summer."[54] The cricket's sound is also heard by other parts of creation, such as "mice" and "the blind lightning," from their birth to their death.[55] The cricket, the original, enters as a reminder of our beginnings, and, with an all-encompassing swing, Merwin extends the message to present and future: "the death of the cricket / is still the cricket / in the bare room the luck of the cricket / echoes."[56]

Given the spare language, the numinous presentation of events and images, and a paradoxical ending (how, in death, can the cricket still be the cricket?), it is difficult to be certain that a clear attitudinal reversal of the agonized Merwin of *The Lice* has occurred. Does the "luck" of the cricket indicate any luck at all for the listeners? Luckiness or unluckiness is not implied for the living, but rather, in the poet's puzzling twists of language, existence remains ultimately an enigma. Only the cricket, as origin, is left sounding within the "bare room" of the world, and if we are aware it may help us establish a sense of ourselves as earthly citizens. The continuous voice of this cricket evokes similar sounds from Keats's "On the Grasshopper and Cricket." In both, the singers vocalize when silence has overtaken the scene; they signify the voices of presence above absence, and, especially in Keats's poem, the voice is indicative of ongoing life: "The poetry of earth is ceasing never."[57]

In another poem using an animal or an animal-like spirit, Merwin tries to throw off the restrictions of civilization and return to an original self. "Lemuel's Blessing," from *The Moving Target*, gives us a narrator who feels as confined as a domestic dog in his daily living but who wants to have the freedom of the wolflike spirit that he addresses. He admires the spirit and wants to learn from him:

> You that know the way,
> Spirit,
> I bless your ears which are like cypruses on a mountain
> With their roots in wisdom. Let me approach.[58]

The ways of civilization are perceived as traps, and in naming these traps one by one the narrator prays that he will be able to escape the constructs of humans and live like the wolf who answers to no person and no set of rules:

> Deliver me
>
> From the ruth of the lair, which clings to me in the morning,
> Painful when I move, like a trap;

Even debris has its favorite positions but they are not yours;
From the ruth of kindness with its licked hands;[59]

The speaker regrets having given in to the demands of history, which he sees as having used his body for its own purposes. He wishes the wolf to serve as his model and guardian spirit, so that he may free himself and obtain the strength that the wolf has to endure in the wilderness. The laws of civilization, that enclose humans in a system where individuality is snuffed out, are tantamount to losing one's own body. By praying to this genuine being, there is hope of maintaining what is left of the real:

Preserve my eyes, which are irreplaceable.
Preserve my heart, veins, bones,
Against the slow death building in them like hornets until the place
  is entirely theirs.[60]

The eyes are "irreplaceable" because they represent the individual's vision of life, and the risk of death or failure does not bother the speaker to the same degree as loss of self. To have experience dictated or mediated by systems of behavior destroys the individual, as surely, as the speaker says, as "the ruth of known paths, which would use my feet, tail, and ears as curios, / ... My fate as a warning."[61] His single legacy will be his "cry stretched out behind [him] like a road."[62] The inarticulate cry, the howl in the wilderness, becomes, strangely for this most erudite of poets, indicative of the primal world he valorizes in frustration over the crimes and repressions of his own society. "Lemuel's Blessing" is a relatively early poem—from 1963—and its message reflects more the problems of society than how a holistic vision may solve those problems. However, it demonstrates an incipient process in Merwin of looking toward the natural world for insight, a process that must be ongoing and evolving like the living world itself.

As we can see from Merwin's poetry, animals are central to our earth and to our ability to properly conceive the rest of earth. Mark Christhilf points out that Merwin believes that even though we try to abolish the connection between ourselves and the animals, we are never truly successful. Animals, like other components of origin, exist within the unconscious, prior to our history. As proof that this Jungian concept resides in Merwin, Christhilf cites "Lemuel's Blessing," where knowledge of the original being exists within the narrator's pysche and pushes its way to the surface.[63] Unfortunately, however, our rationalizations usually take over. The animals found in Merwin's early poetry, primarily, the bestiary in *Green with Beasts*, reflect our desire to see ourselves in the animals, to bring one more part of the natural world into our domain. In these poems, humans' endeavors to impress ourselves on the environment and to psychically absorb it are at issue. We fail when we try to anthropomorphize, when we attempt to use animals as a mirror to ourselves. For the modern ecothinker, the position should be one of recognizing shared attributes as well as differences and not ascribing the humanlike to animals in order to validate them through a sort of narcissism.

This bibliohistory represents a progression of Merwin's ideas on the subject as his career progressed. After his criticism of our mental appropriation of the animals comes his poetry expressing the longing to derive from them what can legitimately be ours—not ownership but kinship. Merwin continues in the 1970s to condemn humankind's arrogance and abuse, but the wellspring of selfhood—origin—offers a reacquaintance with our relation with the animals. Perhaps one of the most joyful poems in this category is "The Paw," from *The Carrier of Ladders*. "The Paw" presents us with a speaker who returns to his primal self with the help of his counterpart, a female wolf. Merwin's idea for such an essentialist experience may have derived from the South American and Mesoamerican concept of nagualism, also found, less frequently, among North American Native cultures. Åke Hult-krantz defines the nagual as a guardian animal or species of animal intimately connected to an individual, which may have originally been restricted to shamans and socially powerful persons.[64] Hultkrantz describes the closeness of the human and animal in nagualism, which relates them psychically and physically:

> It is sometimes called the "alter ego" concept, due to the intense identifica-tion of the individual with his guardian spirit, so much so that in certain situations it can become the exponent of his own ego. . . . In nagualism are found in condensed form all those characteristics in a guardian spirit by which it is linked to man: if the nagual is strong and powerful, so is its protégé; if one of them is wounded, so is the other, and in the same part of the body; if one of them dies, the other dies too. The Indian may change into his guardian spirit, at least if he is a shaman, and in that form travel far, for example, to the land of the dead.[65]

With the closeness of nagual and protégé, the speaker and the she-wolf, Perdita, experience their reunion through a visit to the primal world:

I return to my limbs with the first
gray light
and here is the gray paw under my hand
the she-wolf Perdita
has come back

. . . . . .

we are coursing the black sierra once more
in the starlight[66]

At the return of his original self and his original counterpart, the
speaker feels the blood returning to his body as well as he feels his
mate: "and there is blood / against my ribs again," while their running
over the landscape creates "wound[s]" from having been opened up
again into life.[67] The narrator's repeated mentioning of the two of
them sharing the same blood, along with their sharing of wounds
(even though Merwin uses these in a regenerative sense) lies very
close to nagualism. The narrator and the she-wolf approach a merging,
and as their senses join, the marriage is welcomed that will bring
them to a genuine life.

With Merwin, inhibiting and even dangerous forces are often present, but the speaker hopes that he can hold on to his and his lover's
experience before their world is extinguished. The two appear to
narrowly make their escape "before the stars fall / and the mountains
go out / and the void wakes / and it is day."[68] In this poem, it seems
imperative that the two make their escape together, for whatever time
is left on the earthly clock. As in nagualism, if the animal guardian
is captured, so is the human subject. This is one of the few poems in
which Merwin will allow an unmitigated return to origin and seems
to be at home with this message. The return is made all the more
real because it is accomplished through the animal world and through
a mythic framework that recognizes the need for living spiritual
connections between humankind and nature. Even twenty-six years
later, Merwin offers a Perdita-like character in his 1996 volume, *The
Vixen*, with the title poem's subject. The vixen is symbol and possessor
of truths that seem in the modern context archaic and obscure:
"Comet of stillness princess of what is over / . . . keeper of the kept
secrets / of the destroyed stories the escaped dreams the sentences."[69]
Like the narrator of "The Paw," the speaker longs in the last moment
for the encounter that will bring understanding and wholeness, the
moment of the vixen again darting over the the wall, before the living
world is exterminated and "the woods are figures."[70] The maxims

of the past lie dead in our historical progressions and ecological uncertainty; language itself appears to have disintegrated. However, the "stories" of the vixen are myth, which is, in effect, an expression of belief in the enduring quality of the world. Myth circumscribes origin, and through myth the narrator may experience a regeneration of language and of life. When he apocalyptically prays for his words to find their home "in the silence after the animals," he is nevertheless desperately struggling for both.[71]

Within Merwin's mythography, totemism, a belief similar to that of the nagual, also finds a place. Totemism is typically defined as a mysterious relationship between an animal or plant species or some other natural phenomena and a generally fictitious kinship group. By this definition, totemism is commonly found among North and South American Indians and in the Old World, although with great diversity. In North America, it frequently carries a taboo against killing the animal with which the clan is associated.[72]

"Words from a Totem Animal" is narrated by such a figure, but the animal-spirit expresses not his unity with humankind but his wish to be delivered by the "god of beginnings" into a more genuine life.[73] The totem animal appears to be caught between what he considers as fruitful lives; he is a spirit who is sought by humans for aid, but playing a part in the world of humans is not what he was meant for.

The totem animal says that he might have been able to exist within the humans' world of "walls" and "reasons," but now his original desire for freedom is exerting itself—"the old trees jump up again and again"—and he cannot stay a human icon:

> Caught again and held again
> again I am not a blessing
> they bring me
> names
> that would fit anything
> they bring them to me
> they bring me hopes
> all day I turn
> making ropes
> helping[74]

The totem animal perceives that the "one sound" that could lift his confusion is trailing him from world to world, but his death (or banishment to the spirit world) prevents him from hearing it on every occasion. Thus, we have a poem that receives its dramatic intensity from the division that a spirit feels from his true nature, rather than Merwin's usual division of human from nature. Interestingly enough, however, the totem animal's sense of anxiety and loss are the same sorts of feelings that Merwin's humans have when they recognize their division. When the totem animal verbalizes his fear, he describes himself as losing his animal nature and becoming like a human:

> I dreamed I had no nails
> no hair
> I had lost one of the senses
> not sure which
> the soles peeled from my feet and
> drifted away[75]

The singular element in the universe that has not been "used," that has not had a label put upon it and thereby had its original nature compromised, is "silence," which comes as a "blessing / calling me when I am lost."[76] Even the stars have been thoroughly schematized, leaving only the nonentity of silence as a refuge from the smothering of the soul.

The final hope of the totem animal is that he will receive unification with his original self at some future time: "Maybe I will come / to where I am one / ... as a new / year finds the song of the nuthatch."[77] His wish is for another life, like his original one, "because this one is growing faint."[78] Before we leave the poem, we must ask ourselves just what Merwin is saying about the world by way of Native mythos. The culprit, of course, is not mythos, New World or other, but the nearly unbridgeable gaps between humanity and the rest of the biotic community when anthropocentric misconceptions deny our place in that community. Merwin's choice of the totem animal is quite clever. From his poetry and translations he unmistakably admires myth. Here, he turns a symbol on its ear, and human frailties are expressed through a figure that otherwise would represent a familial bond to nature.

The poems that we have looked at in this chapter are by no means the only ones that involve animals and original longings. "Horse," "Little Horse," and "Animals from Mountains" are a few of the others that evoke this facet of naturism. Animals represent our closest ties to origin because they are most like us. Yet, the recognition that we are different from them in order to avoid the danger of anthropomorphization, and thereby appropriation, is also not ignored by Merwin's ecological lyrics. The poet's strongest expressions involving an original world are found in the books of the seventies—*The Carrier of Ladders, Writings to an Unfinished Accompaniment,* and *The Compass Flower.* Most noticeably, the long love poem found in *The Compass Flower,* "Kore," revolves around the desire to return to an original world. However, the concept appears in other books as well and often in his collections of prose poems, *The Miner's Pale Children* and *Houses and Travellers,* also published during the seventies. These poems illustrate the hope for return; they are Merwin's most regular songs of joy. Stemming from this project, however, is the alternate sense of grief from having lost a unified life, the representation of the dystopia engendered by the modern machine.

Division

I<small>N AN ESSAY ENTITLED "THE FORMS OF WILDNESS," HAYDEN WHITE ASSERTS</small> that the perception of society as a fall away from a natural perfection, from a providential rather than a savage nature, can be found in John Locke, Edmund Spenser, Baron de Montesquieu, and Jean-Jacques Rousseau, among others.[1] This dislocation is evident in Merwin, where the postmodern American situation manifests the problem sometimes to the extreme. In the two centuries since Rousseau, the space between humankind and the providential nature described by White seems to have jumped by leagues. Now technoculture is creating conditions that can isolate large populations from any sustained contact with plants, animals, or even the atmosphere. Vexed with the loss of nature in our lives and the loss of an original self, Merwin has produced several poems on the subject. To Merwin, the epistemological and physical distance between ourselves and nature that we have increasingly created has divided us from our most important psychic resource and the basis of our being. Humans are a part of a collective universe, and by shaping the world to accommodate our immediate desires we have gone far to eliminate the original conditions that we need for a complete, healthy environment. Whether we are living in a metropolis or in a rural area, it is likely, in our contemporary state, that we have little knowledge of the natural area in which we live and have even less contact with it on an experiential, daily level.

Egocentrism has helped lead to "forgetting," a key problem with Merwin's humans. An original self once existed, a self that was in harmony with the universe and was a positive, functioning part of it. However, with the advance of human knowledge and pride has come a decline in original understanding. As we have become more and more separate from the natural world with our buildings and technological creations, recognition of the origin becomes less likely. At times, "forgetting" is a positive word in the Merwin dictionary because it entails the forgetting of useless and often destructive human modes of thought. Yet, the forgetting of origin is the forgetting of part of ourselves and has made people less than whole.

Modern human beings especially are fractured selves, divided from their beginnings and the ecosystem that has managed to survive around them, although it exists in great danger. Without daily experience in the living world and without seeing ourselves as part of a larger physical context, there is nothing to sustain Merwin's humans. Compounding the problem is our own ignorance of what has caused our rootlessness, which in turn prevents us from seeking to reestablish former biotic bonds. *Book VI* of William Wordsworth's *The Prelude*, "Residence in London," describes a sense of chaos amid urban clutter and distraction from natural unity. Wordsworth's city blinds the eye by captivating its onlookers, by obstructing the vision of the natural; in Merwin it is more closely the "modern" that obfuscates the "original."

To be specific about the poetry I am including under the category "division," I would like to define the division poems as those works which lament or long for a lost, original world while emphasizing our present ideological distance from it. Only a selected group of Merwin's poems meet these criteria, yet I believe that they are vital to the development of Merwin's outlook toward nature and his poetic attitude in general. Another thread, which presents a world of voids, of humans cut off spiritually from the phenomenal world (with no implications of an origin of which we were once a part), has probably generated more criticism on Merwin than anything else. We find these poems repeatedly in the second four books—*The Moving Target, The Lice, The Carrier of Ladders,* and *Writings to an Unfinished Accompaniment.* Emptiness, alienation, and their synonyms became, in the sixties and early seventies, a popular topic in essays about Merwin. Yet, the poet's hopeful moments are often recorded in these books and grew markedly within the time frame, making the temper of these volumes not easily definable.

The more recent criticism of Edward Brunner and Mark Christhilf attests to this ambiguity. The poems of division, like the scattered poems of origin we find in these books, indicate Merwin's desire for his own reestablishment of natural ties, a renewal that was necessary for the production of the belief-filled *The Compass Flower* in 1977. Merwin is and never has been an apologist for humankind or for his own fire-and-brimstone ecohomiletics. If there is division, it is because humans have made it so. Yet, because the living world still exists, there is the possibility for overcoming division to some extent. However, before we jump ahead to possibility, let us examine the reasons we have drifted away from origin.

As Merwin's poetry of an original world moves temporally backward to what must be called prehistory, so do his poems of division. By imaginatively constructing a single and distinct initial moment of the psychic severing of the human/nature ties, division is shown as a conscious act in "Beginning" from *The Carrier of Ladders*. It is no accident to have befallen humankind. In an interesting twist of imagery, Merwin uses a natural object, a crane, to beckon humans to exercise their power to order the world in their own way. The "king of the black cranes" arises on a white landscape "Long before spring," or before the first spring has ever come about.[2] The white landscape in juxtaposition to the blackness of the bird points to the degree of the impending differences between humankind and the natural world. The crane observes the scene with his turning head and justifies the imposition of his (and humans') ego upon it. When the crane's survey determines that on the polarlike surface north lies in all directions, the possibilities for human domination are unlimited: "the crown turns / and the eye / drilled clear through his head / turns / it is north everywhere / come out he says."[3]

The call to humans to "come out" represents our own ambition calling to itself. Satirically, Merwin tells us that the world is full of potential for conquest if only we will leave behind our inhibitions. Our inhibitions, which may better be called respect, give way to larger goals as history records. The final directive of the crane is for humans to come forward with their civilization and to bring with them their "nights," or those darker parts of the psyche that obviously cannot be left behind.[4] "Nights" here stands in opposition to the whiteness of the landscape in the same way that the black crane does. The "beginning" that serves as the title is ironically no beginning to be wished for but the beginning of the end. (Ironies, turnarounds, and twists, we should observe, are as much a part of Merwin's technique as are his noted ellipses and spareness of language). "Beginning" goes about handling the issue of division in a unique way, because, typically, the poet muses upon division long after it has begun and when its remedy seems nearly impossible. In this poem, the foundations of our current situation are delineated. With arrogance and opportunity we have both controlled and divided ourselves from the natural world.

However, another sort of opportunity does exist, the opportunity for recovery, at least in part.

The chance for restoring original knowledge exists because of the presence of images and elements that bind us to nature. "Bread," from *Writings to an Unfinished Accompaniment*, offers physical realities from the life of the earliest humans as a forgotten knowledge of modern humankind. In primitive life, humans had natural places for shelter, and the narrator ponders whether the directionless people he passes on the street can have completely left behind these early bonds: "have they forgotten the pale caves / they dreamed of hiding in / their own caves / full of the waiting of their footprints."[5] The "bread" that early humankind sought was something that nourished them in a spiritual manner—"the heart of bread / to be sustained by its dark breath."[6] The risk the poet runs, and, runs into, is that for most readers "caves" conjures unpleasant associations with darkness, dampness, and the unknown. The cave imagery, I believe, fails on the emotive level because of its eeriness. Yet, in a striking coincidence where Thoreau mourns the obstruction of nature by buildings, he relates caves to our primal selves: "Who does not remember the interest with which when young he looked at shelving rocks, or any approach to a cave? It was the natural yearning of that portion of our most primitive ancestor which still survived in us."[7] Merwin's "The Horizons of Rooms" offers a similar context with a similar reference to memory: "the first room was made of stone and ice / and a fallen tree // . . . once there is a room / we know there was something before."[8]

Unique about "Bread" in comparison to other division poems is that it is not essentially a vocal critique of society. Primarily, a primitive yet vital life is depicted in detail for its value alone. The poem's closing stanza offers one of the most romantic images we can find in Merwin—humans are pictured "alone / before a wheat field / raising its radiance to the moon."[9] I cite this stanza not as a standard representation of the poet's attitude, but rather as evidence of Merwin's belief in the deep-rooted need of human beings to live as a part of the original natural framework.

That there are tangible factors still connecting us to the original world gives us further reason to make the case that in Merwin's poetry industrial and postindustrial loss has not borne utter hopelessness. Merwin spoke of his belief in a unity of experience, along with its relationship to poetry, at a 1989 poetry festival:

I think that the thing that poetry has in common with all the arts is it's an expression of faith in the integrity of the senses and of the imagination. And these are what we have in common with the natural world. The animals have no doubt about the integrity of their senses, you know, they're essential to them. And whatever the animal imagination may be, we can imagine it as being connected with their senses. And ours is too. ... life is a whole and that we are a part of it, and we must never ever forget that. And the thing that comes out of that, the only things in many of our urban lives that still come out of that are our dreams, some of our erotic life, if we're lucky, and any sensual experience that we can still find faith in and we can still believe in.[10]

In the poems of division, Merwin will sometimes imaginatively present nature actively endeavoring to restore original connections with humankind. "The Current" and "The Clear Skies" best depict this situation. Yet, despite the overtures from nature, humans are generally stubborn. In the same way that our ego precipitated the schism from origin, we deny any original voices. We have convinced ourselves that the order we have imposed upon the world is of a superior kind and that we no longer require the voices of the past, especially of such an early past. In contrast to the purity of nature sought by Merwin, A. R. Ammons's *Garbage* immerses the reader in a context of the biological and microbiological. The original, or idyllic, is not a factor in Ammons's realistic representations of natural phenomena: "take, in leavetaking, the leavings: feed your / bony dog, your cat stalking stiff in hunger-meows: / gather up the scraps for pig-swill: anything / thrown out to the chickens will be ground fine / in gizzards or taken underground by beetles and / ants: ..."[11] Loss of a better world does not seem to be an issue for Ammons because all is reducible to the microsystem—that is, until manipulation of the physical interferes with its basic workings: "nothing / much can become of the clear-through plastic / lid: it finds hidden security in the legit / museums of our desecrations ..."[12]

When asked a question about his possible relation to a poet more known for his treatment of anthropocentrism—Robinson Jeffers—Merwin answered with a statement linking our human value to the way in which we value the ecosystem:

The one thing I feel close to is his sense of our self-importance as a species, which I think is one of the things which is strangling us, our own bloated species-ego. The assumption that human beings are different in kind and in importance from other species is something I've had great difficulty in accepting for 25 years or so. To me, it's a dangerously wrong way of seeing things. . . . If we make the distinction in a too self-flattering way, if we say we are the only kind of life that's of any importance, we automatically destroy our own importance. Our importance is based on a feeling of responsibility and awareness of all life. . . .[13]

Thus, the effort we as a society need to put forth is perhaps of the most difficult variety; what is needed is a change in our way of perceiving our place in the world. In the poems of division, the narrators hear the voice of origin, which comes quietly. These speakers are able to hear the voice precisely because they recognize the proper role of humankind in the universe. A balanced sense of the human/ nature mix is achievable, but this sense often conflicts with beliefs that are more comfortable. For whatever reasons—religious, political, economic, or simply as a need we have ascribed to the ego—nature has been psychologically separated from human life and put into service for our imagined gain.

If any one volume illustrates the concept of division, that would be *Writings to an Unfinished Accompaniment,* from which we have already examined "Bread." Numerous other poems from the volume—"The Clear Skies," "The Current," "The Distances," "Looking Back," and "Spring"—unmistakably deal with this topic. Particularly focusing on the conscious refusal of humans to acknowledge origin is "The Clear Skies." Clouds in the poem represent a part of the world that we could once see and see by: "The clouds that touch us out of clear skies // they are eyes that we lost / long ago on the mountain."[14] As humans, we make excuses for the division by deeming ourselves modern and denying our need for the natural: "and because we lose them we say they are old / because they are blind we say / that they cannot find us."[15] In "The Current," our ignorance may not be quite as volitional, yet the result of indifference is the same. Stuck in a mire, we "lie in the marshes like dark coats / forgetting that we are water," but the impressions of "eels" in the "mud" of our psyches spell out our true "names."[16]

Our ideology represented in the division poems has further implications by forming the basis for the destruction of the natural world in the poet's environmental poems. If we do not regret the rift between ourselves and nature, then how can we feel any compunction about altering or annihilating it? Both "The Current" and "The Clear Skies" reveal the first step in a way of viewing the world that will lead not just to separation and loss for humans but also to the depletion of the planet. Human logic, deified by its authors, often fails in not recognizing its limits. For modern humans, this self-certainty perpetuates the state of division: "because we have lost whoever / they are calling / we say that they are not calling / us."[17] As the "clouds" try to reestablish communication with humans, so a "thin cold current" in the self is always awake and is constantly being called to by origin: "then cloud fish call to it again / your heart is safe with us // bright fish flock to it again touch it."[18] The tragedy of both poems is that we refuse to listen. In "The Current," the stream that signified original selfhood ultimately becomes the waters of forgetfulness and of destruction when ignored: "yes and black flukes wave to it / from the Lethe of the whales."[19]

However, Merwin's poetic device of having nature "call" to humankind is blatantly an anthropomorphization. Is there any justification for a poet ever engaging in such an enterprise? In these poems this technique appears to effectively connect us to elements we might not otherwise empathize with; it offers them a "life" we are largely unable to recognize because of our own perceptual idiosyncrasies. Yet, thankfully, Merwin uses this device sparingly, for the dangerous ground of personification—endowing animals or objects with human characteristics—may easily slip into misrepresentation, even with the best of intentions. When an author employs this practice, he admits that he is bestowing his own consciousness upon the subject, and however reasonable the created image may appear, however seemingly compatible with the real object's own "best interests," future reassessments may debunk his assumptions, potentially in the extreme.

As we consider perceptions, Walt Whitman, again, will serve as a "nature" poet whose outlook provides another window to the variant modes of naturism available. In Whitman's poetry the division of the modern world does not exist. Whitman's address to the sea in *Song of Myself* may best demonstrate the difference between Merwin's attitudes about our relationship to the planet and the attitudes of poets like Whitman who find no barriers: "Sea of the brine of life! Sea of unshovelled and always-ready graves! / Howler and scooper of storms! Capricious and dainty sea! / I am integral with you. . . . I too am of one phase and of all phases."[20] Here, we can see a fundamental conceptual difference between Merwin and Whitman. Merwin cannot typically declare that he is at "one" with the world; unity remains an ideal. Just as important, although nature may occasionally try to beckon us in Merwin's poems, a pathetic fallacy on his part, it never depends on a human mate for completion as Whitman would have it: "Earth of the limpid gray of clouds brighter and clearer for my sake! / Far-swooping elbowed earth! Rich apple-blossomed earth! / Smile, for your lover comes!"[21]

To Whitman, the "clouds" are all the more vivid for his "sake," a statement that indicates a dependency of the earth upon the human, that the earth needs humanity to make it come alive. Although we as humans do require the rest of nature for our physical and psychic lives, to assume our presence as necessary for its existence or condition is, in Merwin's ethos, a fault of the ego. As the history of the environment has shown, the supposed primacy of the human above all other things ultimately perceives the world as a tool for our own uses. Whitman praises nature, but it is nature seen through his eye, and the continent he extols, with its increasing population and increasing industry, is essentially a projection of the human mind. Thomas Byers claims that Whitman's technique of cataloging nature in one respect lists "commodities" available rather than "beloved others."[22] For many readers, Whitman's embrace of earth is a valid mode—his bodily desire for eco-union, which expresses itself in prolific, vivid imagery, a genuine manifestation of a writer whose immanentist impulse overshadows any signs of arrogation. However we choose to appraise Whitman, it is plain that the two writers perceive the biosphere in distinct ways.

Often, our anthropocentrism may be witnessed through our relationship to animals. "From many turnings / between the ways of men / and men" the animals in "Shoe Repairs" are ultimately divested of their being and arrayed on racks.[23] Yet, Merwin reminds us of their former lives and with an atypical pun—"soles" (souls)—seems to conjure up for them an original existence equal to any human native society: "soles / eyes of masks / from a culture lost forever."[24] The comparison, no doubt, is intended to weaken mental demarcations between ourselves and the animals; we are meant to understand that theirs was once a life among their own kind, too. However, again, these comparisons anthropomorphize the animals, the same practice Merwin condemns in *Green with Beasts*. Although this device does not defeat the poem's impact, it nevertheless restricts the animals to our own paradigms, and the tropes would have been better left out.

Ultimately, the poem shifts us into an imagined future. Using Noah's ark, Merwin projects a scene where humans, shoeless, remember the animals we once extinguished: "We will know the smell / in another life / stepping down / barefoot into this Ark."[25] The ark to come will be devoid rather than full of animals: "seeing it lit up but empty," and although we have put them into our own false couplings, they nevertheless will have died "each alone."[26] The prophecy here concerns humankind as well as the animals. We will be the losers when thought-lessness has taken us to the point of eliminating our closest relatives on the planet. So the message is not for a fictional future, but for the present day. The "ways of men" with which we cannot see the animals except as something to use and with which we cannot envision them as any sort of group with their own right to existence creates the opportunity for abuses.

Some readers have charged that the poems of Merwin often fall into didacticism. In the case of the poems of division and the poems of environment (which "Shoe Repairs" both partakes of) they are correct. However, it is a charge Merwin obviously is willing to accept because he continues to write explicitly on these issues.

Numerous critics have noted the postapocalyptic situation of much of Merwin's poetry, and this is an important characteristic of the poems of division. In most of these poems, ages have apparently contributed to the psychic space between humans and nature, and the narrator is left to reflect upon the outcome. Like a survivor of a faraway disaster who can relate only the facts of the event in his tale, the speaker, in contrast to his society, has knowledge of the import of the tragedy, but little or nothing can be done for its rectification. Nevertheless, with the inclusive pronouns "we" and "us" usually used in these poems, the speaker admits his own complicity as a member of the society perpetuating these attitudes. It is by telling the tale, by a public confession of humankind's wrongdoing—that is, by the poem itself—that the poet discloses his hope. Few poems will be found that overtly offer promise—"my mind infinitely divided and hope-less"—"dust gathers all day on our closed lids"—typify the locutions of the narrators.[27] Yet, the mere fact that this loss is important enough to recite over and over, about and for the society we are in, reveals an implicit desire and chance for restoration.

Merwin's concern for humanity is that we have created an environment that is becoming more and more hostile to us and is more and more depleted of value. Like the passenger on an airliner in "Plane," "We hurtle forward and seem to rise," but our journey is only toward loss.[28] Modern technology would do away with all mythology, which would ground humankind in something larger than the self: "where is no / vision of the essential nakedness of the gods / nor of that / nakedness the seamless garment of heaven" and simply leave us with the "air."[29] Nature as progenitor has been dethroned; it is as if we have formed ourselves and our planet. "Plane" illustrates what Wendell Berry terms "the machine metaphor."[30] Now that we, in modern times, have placed ourselves in charge of creation, it has been reduced to the equivalent of a raw material for use by our machines: "The Modern World would respect the Creation only insofar as it could be *used* by humans. . . . By means of the machine metaphor we have eliminated any fear or awe or reverence or humility or delight or joy that might have restrained us in our use of the world."[31] Berry also notes the participation of premodern peoples in the cycles of life and death, as we saw in the closing stanza of "Bread," where the circle of human, earth, and universe constituted a real and a mystical foundation for living.[32] In contrast, Berry states, "Our 'success' is a catastrophic demonstration of our failure. The industrial Paradise is a fantasy in the minds of the privileged and the powerful; the reality is a shambles."[33]

These dystopian statements well summarize many of Merwin's opinions on our modern condition. Living in climate-controlled buildings, transporting ourselves by machines, and comunicating by electronics, we have pushed away the need for any sense of mystery about the natural world and the need for knowledge of our essential place within it. Merwin would agree with J. Hector St. John de Crève-coeur's eighteenth-century dictum in *Letters from an American Farmer* that "Men are like plants; the goodness and flavour of the fruit proceeds from the peculiar soil and exposition in which they grow."[34] Further, the environmental loss in *The Lice* and *The Rain in the Trees* demonstrates the real-world consequences of this split. Yet, our lives still contain original connections and always will contain these connections because we are aspects of nature, and this, too, finds its place in the poetry. Merwin's despair falters at moments when conscious effort can restore the vision of origin: "the eye must burn again and again / through each of its lost moments / until it sees."[35]

Despite its dangers and despite an already-established logging trade, the wilderness that Thoreau encountered in 1846 in *The Maine Woods* surprisingly resembles Merwin's distant origin. Traveling the rivers and lakes of backwoods Maine to Mount Ktaadn, Thoreau describes the impact upon him of one setting he encountered:

The little rill tinkled the louder, and peopled all the wilderness for me; and the glassy smoothness of the sleeping lake, laving the shores of a new world, with the dark, fantastic rocks rising here and there from its surface, made a scene not easily described. It has left such an impression of stern, yet gentle, wildness on my memory as will not soon be effaced.[36]

The world Thoreau presents is "new" and alive, and its "wildness" is the root of its wonder. If this nineteenth-century portrait resembles Merwin's ideal, his "origin" (and from his sense of following in the writer's tradition, I believe that there is good reason for such supposition), it is easy to understand Merwin's dismay at the modern movement away from this state toward an increasingly sterile technocracy.

In "Plane," we noted the absence of human belief in the worth of nature as entity and our existence within the artificial environments we have created—the viscious circle engendering the psychic division that leaves humans out of touch with themselves as well as the ecosystem. "Airport," from *The Rain in the Trees*, depicts another jet-age subject as a paradigm for the modern situation and describes what happens to people living in this context. The hallmark of the airport is its impersonality. Even the human contact that one may find there is no more personal than that which a machine could give. The "facility," which is "devoted to absence in life," leads people out of it through "chute[s]," after which a person smiles at the ticket, not the traveler, and directs him to a seat.[37] Driven through passages like manufactured objects, humans essentially lose all contact with one another. The airport is no real place but a function tragically representative of the mechanisms of much of the contemporary world. It is not lived in but "serviced"; it is a structure filled with "signs" and does nothing more than execute "a process."[38]

The purpose of the airport is to deliver people somewhere else, and the experience of having been through the airport leaves no memory, but only emptiness: "we travel far and fast / and as we pass through we forget / where we have been."[39] As in T. S. Eliot's poem, this technological wasteland reflects itself in the lives of the people who move through it. Throughout all of Merwin's volumes since *The Moving Target*, wandering, in search of enlightenment or as a symptom of aimlessness, has been a central motif. Yet, nowhere more than in poems like "Airport" does this act generate such tragic consequences. Movement now becomes a fruitless task, unlike the spiritual journeys toward origin.

Merwin has also spoken of another modern facility, the supermarket, as emblematic of our division from nature. Like the airport, the supermarket gives humans nothing to connect with in any sensual or emotional way:

> You go into a supermarket and what do you have, you have artificial light, you have canned music, you have deodorant, everything's deodorized, everything's in boxes, out of—you can't touch it, you can't taste it, you can't smell it, you can't see it, and you can't hear anything except what they want you to hear. And no wonder everybody wanders around like a zombie, because your senses have been sort of taken away from you for a while, you know. And I think that's kind of an intensification of the society we live in. A supermarket is kind of, you know, the whole thing brought into a focus. That's what it's about, isn't it, selling you things? . . . These things are there, they don't belong there, they didn't grow there. . . . This is a very strange kind of situation, but it's kind of typical of our lives.[40]

Perhaps the poem that best describes what has become of humans who live in the impersonal and unnatural milieu of airports and supermarkets is "Glasses." Having lived so long in the artificial, people behave mechanically and no actions seem to have any more meaning than others. In fact, their behavior is so dehumanized, Merwin deliberately conflates them with the glass doors that they live behind: "they are real glass and thin."[41] The poem pictures contemporary humans as characteristically having no interest in the world—natural or unnatural—about them. Adding a political dimension to the poem, the same people who are dissociated from the natural environment are making decisions about it by voting, a schism that is underscored by their ignorance of the "stars turn[ing]" "around them."[42] Learning and defending the landforms, flora, fauna, and native culture of the area in which we live—what Gary Snyder calls "bioregional" awareness—would begin to solve the problems described here.[43] As Snyder explains, bioregionalism finally offers geographical areas their chance to be considered in the political process: "Bioregionalism is the entry of place into the dialectic of history."[44] Furthermore, bioregionalism is not simply for rural enlightenment and preservation—it is as much concerned with the restoration of urban neighborhoods and the "greening" of our cities.[45] Ecologically, cities can be reclaimed to a surprising extent. Relative ecological equilibrium is attainable in our urban centers with proper environmental controls and the integration of adopted natural areas, such as parks, gardens, and even lawns. An urban lake, stream, or woodland can be maintained, as closely as possible, in its original condition, supporting native plants and wildlife.

In the city from "Glasses," what all too realistically motivates its contemporary citizens is money, not consciousness about what is happening to the planet, to their home, or to other people. These typical "modern" humans control the machines that shape the world at their will and live without regret, despite the consequences:

> they go on wheels they are without color
> they come in clothes out of closets
> they fly above the earth reading papers
> the bulldozers make way for them[46]

Atypically, this poem repetitively uses a third-person pronoun—"they"—but we understand that the subjects are, in reality, ourselves. The division poems do not indicate much hope that we will try to divest ourselves of the barriers—the physical obstructions and the perceived distances—that we have established between our lives and the natural world. Our membership in the planet, absent of global concern and bioregional focus, has become tenuous to the point of extinction, and the poet's work on environmental loss in *The Lice* and *The Rain in the Trees* demonstrates the real-world danger of not bridging these gaps that we have established. Our lives, however, still contain original connections and always will contain these ties, because, as humans, we not only physically but psychically require the natural world in our lives. In the next two chapters we will see how Merwin employs two techniques, silence and the disembodied narrator, in an attempt to lyrically rediscover first unities.

3

The Disembodied Narrator

To achieve the participation in nature that they desire, Merwin's
narrators betray little or no personal identity and often seem as if
they are voices speaking free of the body. These "disembodied" narrators lack a particular self so that they may make their quests without
the burdens of the ego. In the vast majority of Merwin's poems, their
actions remain part of a journey or process, far from restoration of
origin. However, their efforts are not futile. Disembodiment aids them
in losing realities that are restrictive; that is, it helps them to make
steps toward origin, and it translates the experience more readily to
the reader.

Charles Molesworth notes Merwin's prevalent use of a disembodied
narrative agent and believes that the disembodiment typically appears
figuratively or as a desire toward such a state because the speaker
sees the world as "irremediably fallen, so that to be entangled in
materiality is synonymous with evil."[1] Molesworth also sees this technique as a method of gaining knowledge metaphysically, a knowledge
not available to those in the body. Though I do not agree with Molesworth's estimation that, as he puts it, a "kind of rarified second-
degree allegory" that is unsuccessful runs through Merwin's work,
he nevertheless brings up a valuable point when he notes Merwin's
attempts to remove himself from a physical circumstance that is
imperfect.[2]

One short poem from *The Carrier of Ladders*, "Lark," presents a speaker
who wants to get out of the body, who wants to relieve himself of his
humanity in his desire for a more integrated being and understanding.
Merwin begins the poem by addressing the lark, but by the second
stanza the subject of the wished-for transformation has become the
narrator:

> In the hour that has no friends
> above it

you become yourself
voice
black
star burning in cold heaven
speaking well of it
as it falls from you
upward

Fire
by day
with no country
where and at what height
can it begin
I the shadow
singing I
the light³

The speaker's method of disembodying himself is by taking himself
out of charted time, into "the hour that has no friends," and by taking
himself out of the world and into the "cold heaven," which is no
traditional heaven but another uncharted realm, "no country." Merwin's scheme is to remove the body from spatial and temporal restrictions in order to liberate the self. Although many critics see Merwin's
disembodied voice as yet another manifestation of his sometime
gloom, here and in many other poems the loss of self works toward a
spiritual fulfillment. Yet, the spirituality desired also reflects Merwin's
usual paradoxical mode—he desires to be both "shadow" and "light."
When the speaker ends this future journey out of the self and into
a more direct contact with the universe, we are not quite sure where
he is. Our best prediction of the speaker's future circumstance may
be to say that it will be in no place and in no time. The loss of the
body, the plunge to the essential self, is part of a process, a continually
ongoing effort that seldom finds its end.

Through disembodiment, Merwin tears away nearly everything
from his narrators that would allow us to identify them. Having no
outward identity, the narrators are subsequently liberated to express
their desire to join the self with the universal. Yet, as in "Lark," the
universal that Merwin seeks to attain is sought through only a few
elements of experience at any one moment, as opposed to the universe
that Whitman reaches for, which contains as much as the poet can
enumerate. Merwin attempts his encounters with spareness and concentration; similarities may be drawn to Thoreau and, oddly, to Emily

Dickinson. His process, as of those writers of the nineteenth century, is metaphysical, although his teleology is not.

Part of Merwin's mission here, as Neal Bowers notes, is to imitate myth and avoid the conventions of "the breath, the pulse, or the movements of the mind" that characterize most of his contemporaries. To reach outward situates the self in the universe, rather than the opposite. On the question of structure, Bowers categorizes Merwin as a free-form formalist, observing in one poem that the poet makes ample use of alliteration, assonance, repetition, and self-contained syntactic units.[4]

In this lyrical mode, "Apples" uses only a few images in a surreal manner in the speaker's encounter with the world. We know nothing of the speaker of the poem, whose literal and metaphorical awakening is in a place once inhabited by others and redolent of their ignorance of the meaning of original song:

> Waking beside a pile of unsorted keys
> in an empty room
> the sun is high
>
> what a long jagged string of broken bird song
> they must have made as they gathered there
> by the ears deaf with sleep
> and the hands empty as waves[5]

Remembering the "birds," the speaker strives to discover the means to bring back their song. The birds are keys to a natural world he has lost and whose meaning remains hidden: "I remember the birds now / but where are the locks // when I touch the pile / my hand sounds like a wave on a shingle beach."[6] He realizes that the sounds that he makes are merely echoes, like "someone stirring / in the ruins of a glass mountain / after decades."[7] Or, to phrase it another way, he recognizes his division from the original natural world—the mysterious liminal remembrance of origin.

Understanding comes at the end of the poem, when all the keys to living "melt" with the narrator's touch, except one "to the door of a cold morning / the color of apples."[8] The speaker's link to nature, to an early, mythical world, is slight, but it is present. The "cold morning" contains a "door," a ready symbol of opportunity occurring frequently in Merwin. "Apples" has a well-known classical base in the tale of the golden apples of the Hesperides, as well as a common identification with the fruit of the Eden story. The poem's mythic reverberations allow Merwin to enter into a brief narration without concentration on a local self. A more localized self, surrounded by the specifics of time and place, will appear later, most obviously in the Hawaiian poems in *The Rain in the Trees* (1988) and in poems set in southwest France in *The Vixen* (1996).

A disembodied narrator in "Midnight in Early Spring" also must recognize the remnants of origin among the barrenness of the present. We know nothing more of the narrator than we know of the "us," as he discerns that the happenings around him are omens:

> At one moment a few old leaves come in
> frightened
> and lie down together and stop moving
> the nights now go in threes
> as in a time of danger
> the flies
> sleep like sentries on the darkened panes
>
> some alien blessing
> is on its way to us
> some prayer ignored for centuries
> is about to be granted to the prayerless[9]

That revelation from nature may arrive in awe- or fear-inspiring circumstances has long been a tradition in romantic literature, as evidenced by the famous boat scene from Wordsworth's *Prelude* and the harrowing experiences of Samuel Taylor Coleridge's mariner. Too, Eliot's *The Waste Land* brings this motif to the modern day with the grim landscape of the first section, which later appears as the scene of a soft-spoken prophecy.

In the second half of Merwin's poem, the speaker addresses the revelation as if it were a human: "who were you / cold voice born in captivity / rising / last martyr of a hope . . . last son . . . who were you."[10] His repeated question, "who were you," we could equally ask of the speaker in the present tense with "who are you." However, the speaker is not present in the poem to identify himself. He is there to serve as listener, and as a good listener he knows that original unity must be heard if any liberation in the future is to take place: "so that we may know why / when the streams / wake tomorrow and we are free."[11] Although Merwin seems positive about this restoration, the bulk of his poetry does not indicate that he is convinced of its happening, and we should not infer that he is certain here. Restoration of origin can no more be predicted than the ecological future of the planet. Here, the voice of the ancient complements the apocalyptic position Merwin often takes. In short, we may say that Merwin's poetry is filled with earthly beginnings and endings that have at their root the same purpose. In writing about potential tragic endings, the poet hopes to help to prevent them; in seeking beginnings, he hopes to bring their value to the calamitous present day.

Merwin's desire for union with the world is regarded by Laurence Lieberman as well as Molesworth as a key indicator of the poet's philosophical end. To Lieberman, Merwin's impersonal narrators are evidence of his longing to become "a tool, an instrument, a pure vehicle for the 'one truth,' the vision that suddenly fills the fertile, incubating emptiness" in which the spirit is free from human needs. This freedom is the condition of self-purification and independence that allows for the reception of images from the subconscious mind or from the racial preconscious. Too, Lieberman states, it has its role for Merwin the translator because it establishes a "psychic medium for the poetry of foreign tongues."[12]

The concept of self-emptying in order to attain religious enlightenment and even identification with the "one truth" or deity is common among religions of the East. Contrasting the religions of Judaism, Christianity, and Islam to those of the East, Joseph Campbell remarks that in the latter a principle of identification with the divinity through self-loss is often professed. Loss of self does not lead to negation, but on the contrary, to transcendence:

> Gods and Buddhas, in the Orient are, accordingly, not final terms—like Yahweh, the Trinity, or Allah, in the West—but point beyond themselves to that ineffable being, consciousness, and rapture that is the All in all of us. And in their worship, the ultimate aim is to effect in the devotee a psychological transfiguration through a shift of his plane of vision from the passing to the enduring, through which he may come finally to realize in experience (not simply as an article of faith) that he is identical with that before which he bows.[13]

The individual's "shift of his plane of vision" out of the present and the identification of the self (which is paradoxically suspended) with an original world (which must serve in place of the absent deity) is what Merwin attempts. The end of the effort has necessarily been secularized and "naturalized" for this postmodern poet of the earth, but the concept remains analogous.

The impersonal, lone narrators that Merwin employs are the best vehicles for the delivery of these often prophetic and prayerlike poems. Separate from the everyday world and all of its strictures, Merwin's speakers are something like wandering prophets, able to hear the voice in the desert because they apparently have no strong ties to society. Sometimes, however, although these speakers have made themselves available to such intuition or intimations, they also have a tinge of fatalism about them. Merwin's listeners may seem astonished at finding themselves in their position as readers of the universe. When, in one poem, the narrator says, "This must be what I wanted to be doing, / Walking at night between the two deserts, / Singing," the lines ring with surprise rather than certainty.[14]

Usually, the narrators do appear more willing, and often they are active seekers of knowledge. What stops this poetry short of being truly prophetic is that the narrators generally come away only with intimations rather than large answers. The poems close with the sense of the speakers having acquired a small parcel of knowledge in a world filled with questions. However, the narrators also seem as if they will continue their wandering, holding their small packages.

This standard partial illumination, along with the disembodied speaker, is apparent in "To the Rain" from *Writings to an Unfinished Accompaniment*, where understanding is sought during a shower of rain. As in "Apples," the physical circumstance is described in a fashion as elliptical as the speaker's character. The little that we know of the rain is that it is ancient and that it is colorless and nameless: "You reach me out of the age of the air / clear ... if any of you has a name / it is unknown // but waited for you here / that long / for you to fall through it knowing nothing."[15] The narrator does not identify himself as the one who has "waited" for the rain, nor does he make it clear that he is the one who has known "nothing." This ambiguity, achieved by the dissociation of subject from modifier, contributes to the sketchiness of the speaker. By not giving us the proper connections between himself and his actions in this passage, he appears almost as ephemeral as the rain, and he seems ready to make an ontological move.

Addressing the rain as "hem of the garment"—a reference to the biblical stories of people who touched the hem of Jesus' garment in order to receive healing—and repeating his wish to love what he cannot know, the speaker picks up the personal pronoun again: "hem of the garment / do not wait / until I can love all that I am to know /

for maybe that will never be."[16] Willing to forgo logical and emotional preludes, he admits his self-distrust, and self-loss must take over in order for him to proceed. His admission that he is in a lost state may, through its release of the ego, lead to understanding: "touch me this time / let me love what I cannot know / as the man born blind may love color / until all that he loves / fills him with color."[17] The request for "touch" mixes the language of the body into the poem, but only enough to prevent it from slipping into abstraction.

Questing speakers are common to twentieth-century poetry, yet the particular impersonality of Merwin's figures sets them apart from others. Jarold Ramsey observes that modern parallels to Merwin's searching might be found in Robert Lowell and Theodore Roethke, but that their journeys are influenced by psychological factors, whereas Merwin's are largely free of the personal. Other than the poems about his family that appeared in the fifties and early sixties, Merwin's work largely avoids personal detail but manages to acquire a directness nevertheless.[18] With these poems, we should add a few more (some have appeared since Ramsey's essay)—the family poems in *Opening the Hand*, such as "Sun and Rain" and "Strawberries," and those in *The Rain in the Trees*, such as "The Salt Pond." Although the dominant mode of the middle of our century, the confessionalism of Lowell, Sylvia Plath, and Anne Sexton stands in contrast to Merwin's technique. Whereas Merwin may have his moments of "confession," it would be difficult to imagine his poetry excluding the reach outward.

Instead of characterization, disembodiment is put into play for the directness of experience it allows. As Ramsey states, this impersonality leads to a message with more widespread availability: "Thus the task of self-orientation is made that much more difficult, one would think, but its successful completion in poetry that much more capable of universality of meaning by not being composed of personalized details."[19]

The abandonment of the personal, the self-emptying of Eastern religions also has strong affinities with beliefs of the Native Americans Merwin has studied and translated. In the traditional Native American vision quest, a young man cuts himself loose from the bonds of the tribe and its support in order to experience the spiritual. Charles Alexander Eastman (Ohiyesa), a Santee Sioux of the last generation to be raised in the traditional manner and author of numerous books on the Sioux, relates that the first *hambeday*, or religious retreat of the youth, entailed the individual seeking out the highest summit in a region without bringing material objects other than those of symbolic value.[20] Similarly, in everyday life, "all matters of personal or selfish concern" were considered of the "lower" or "material" mind.[21]

In visionary fashion, Merwin's "Little Horse" presents a speaker in the presence of an archetypal figure from origin. The opening stanzas of "Little Horse" indicate the speaker's longing for origin, his long-felt sense that something unidentifiable has been missing, and a sort of personal "lostness": "You come from some other forest / do you / little horse / think how long I have known these / deep dead leaves / without meeting you // I belong to no one / I would have wished for you if I had known how / what a long time the place was empty."[22] His willingness to meet the horse on its own terms and, as in "Finding a Teacher," to refrain from demanding answers, is the openmindedness that those on a quest must demonstrate: "what can I show you / I will not ask you if you will stay / or if you will come again / I will not try to hold you / I hope you will come with me to where I stand / often sleeping and waking / by the patient water / that has no father nor mother."[23] Merwin's vision may even go so far as to psychically incorporate the individual with the natural as in "The Biology of Art." After looking down into a nameless valley during the "morning" of renewal, the subject "after a long time . . . as water" can "look up."[24]

The processes of exchange of nutrients, water, and vapors among the living beings of the planet and the exchange of elements among the nonliving are real, biochemical transfers constantly being enacted. Plants take up water, but they also release it through transpiration. Plants absorb the soil's nutrients, but these nutrients are returned in the decay of organic matter. Carbon dioxide enters the plant; oxygen exits it. This is but one very simpified sketch of biological exchange, which is to say nothing of transfers—for example, going on within and among soils, the air, rivers, or the subatomic transfers of all matter. Aldo Leopold's 1949 *A Sand County Almanac* describes the journey of an atom before Europeans had set foot on the continent and introduced farming techniques aimed at the cultivation of one species to the exclusion of all others. In this paradigmatic journey, the atom, which Leopold labels "X," travels from rock to flower to acorn to deer to Native American to bluestem to soil to grama (a pasture grass) to buffalo, and onward. In an essay entitled "The Land Ethic," he describes the earth as a circuit with energy and matter merely traveling throughout its passageways, noting that "some energy is dissipated in decay;

some is added by absorption from the air, some is stored in soils, peats and long-lived forests; but it is a sustained circuit, like a slowly augmented revolving fund of life."[25] Leopold's concepts, as those of all environmentalists, embrace a communal structure not evident by superficial examination.

Interaction is vital to the existence of the earth, and not unlike the self-loss of Buddhism or the journey out of the material in the Native American vision quest, Merwin's mythologized disembodiment has as one model the concrete and ongoing movement of molecules. Parts of the planet do not exist in isolation from one another, and psychic at-one-ment with the biotic community also demands fluidity.

The persons whom Merwin chooses to narrate the poems of origin are not as detailed as the specific individuals one might find in a long narrative poem, nor are they the particular egos of the confessional school whose psychological idiosyncrasies we cannot escape. They appear in circumstances that evoke myth, and the search they engage in for origin takes on its own mythic significance. Without the self, without the body, they are free to move through the natural world and seek out its beginnings whose remnants are all they are usually able to discover in a fallen modern world. By being given such disembodied narrators, the reader can more easily transfer his or her own consciousness into the poem than in other poetry where particular egos are identifiable. For poems that are themselves quests, freeing themselves of the body helps to free the speakers of conditions that would restrict them in their efforts.

What is most important, however, is that this journey toward origin, which can be only partially successful, has as its realizable end the orientation of the subject with the natural world. Through its expansion of the speaker's consciousness, the process acts as a sort of earthly initiation. Psychic space is opened and thus knowing. Although this process may appear to some critics as merely rarefication, a phenomenological garden ramble, it reveals the poet's basic need for biotic connections, and it represents a shift in representation from an alienated nature to a giving one. Too, Merwin is setting himself up to take the step into more literal gardens in the volumes of the eighties and nineties. The disembodied speaker is part of his methodology, and silence acts as another key component in his experiment.

Silence

AFTER *THE DRUNK IN THE FURNACE* (1960), HIS FOURTH VOLUME OF POETRY, W. S. Merwin's style shifted from tight, fixed forms and a regular free verse to an explosive style in which lines and stanzas were broken and images appeared in a complex, surrealistic logic. His first two volumes, *A Mask for Janus* and *The Dancing Bears*, were filled with the traditional forms of sestina, carol, ballad, and roundel. Next, with *Green with Beasts* and *The Drunk in the Furnace*, Merwin moved to a more proselike style and often cast these poems in dramatic monologues and what Richard Howard has termed "arguments."[1] Then, with *The Moving Target* came Merwin's most radical change in the language of his poetry. Gone were the elaborate, ornamented tropes of his early career, which were often comprised of archaic and latinate words, and gone were the rather formal speeches. Replacing them was a spare, image-heavy diction that has been widely noted for its use and summoning of silence.

Merwin's philosophical leaning toward the unknown and silence is reflected in this very change. In a 1982 interview, he spoke of his need to change style as evidence of not knowing "what was going to happen next," but knowing that "it wasn't going to be the same thing."[2] To Merwin, the numinousness of experience means that the unknown must be confronted for knowledge to be gained:

> I think that poetry, and maybe all writing, certainly everything we do to some degree, does not come out of what you know, but out of what you don't know. And one of the great superficialities of positivistic thinking is the assumption that things really evolve out of what you know. Nothing evolves out of what you know. You don't move from what you know to something else you know. And it's the unknown that keeps rendering possibilities.[3]

In Merwin's poetry it is usually the sound that is not heard, the word that is not spoken, or the presence that is not seen that allows for meaning. The value of experience must be interpreted, and this interpretation depends upon the imagination to fill in the blank spaces. Critics of Merwin have addressed his silences, absences, and negations probably more than anything else and for good reason. They are pervasive. Yet, to see absence as merely a void is to ignore half of the equation in Merwin's poetry. Beyond the white spaces and negatives often lies the desire for completion. This is the case in his poems dealing with nature, for within them the silences become another vehicle for a truer meeting with origin.

In the same 1982 interview in which Merwin described the value of the unknown, he spoke of the role of listening in writing:

> I think that far more than calculation, deliberate calculation—and a poet begins to smell the kind of writing that comes out of deliberate calculation—what happens with poetry from one poem to the next, from one line to the next, from one word to the next, and certainly from one phase to the next, is much closer to listening for something. You don't know what it is you're listening for, but you recognize it when you hear it. Discipline has a lot to do with it. And also caring about poetry. There are several ways of listening. You can deafen yourself by reading so much and depending on it too much. . . . It's a very tricky business, but I think you spend your whole life learning how to listen. And what you're listening for is something nobody else can hear. So nobody else can tell you how to do it. That's what makes it difficult, what makes it exciting, and what makes it never finished. That means you're always beginning the whole thing.[4]

This belief in listening for the writer translates into the poetry as speakers who immerse themselves in silence in order to hear the genuine. Merwin's speakers are generally alone with the universe, and they are disembodied, but they also often reveal a sense of hope that there is something to listen for. At times, the emptiness and silence offer them nothing, but at other times the echoes of origin are made plain. This is one reason why Merwin's poetry has been so difficult for critics to classify in terms of its attitude, with such critics as Cheri Davis and Mark Christhilf pointing more often to the affirmative end of Merwin's poetry and such critics as Cary Nelson and Anthony Libby pointing more often to Merwin's despair.

If, as Cary Nelson proposes, nature for Merwin "offers us neither consolation nor salvation," we would never see the longing for origin that appears in such poems as "Paw," "Animula," and "Little Horse."[5]

In fact, this hopeful attitude toward the physical world emerges periodically in *The Carrier of Ladders* and becomes dominant by the publication of *The Compass Flower*. Much of the attitude in *The Compass Flower* is a result of its inclusion of love poetry, but, too, the volume is filled with the physical world as a spiritual resource.

This way of looking at nature represents a dramatic shift in the poetry. Two series of poems, the bestiary of *Green with Beasts* and the sea poems of that volume and *The Drunk in the Furnace*, were Merwin's most extensive treatments of nature in his first four books. Essentially, in the first series the failure of humankind to impose its ego upon the animal kingdom is represented, whereas in the latter the sea appears as a nemesis. Following that, poetry in *The Moving Target* and *The Lice* places humankind in an existential quandary with nature and with all of existence, but the primary emphasis lies on despair over history. There, nature seems to offer little to humanity, but humanity's abuses of nature are clearly outlined as part of a collective wrongdoing.

However, Merwin's hopes regarding the natural world grow slowly with the three volumes beginning with *Carrier* and become for him a vital part of his thinking. Gradually, what becomes Merwin's philosophy is the idea that the modern world and communication are essentially failures and that nature holds the value of living. The physical world does still often appear incomprehensible in *The Carrier of Ladders* and the following volume, *Writings to an Unfinished Accompaniment*, but there are just as many moments where Merwin feels that it is nourishing. As time goes on with Merwin, more and more the silences of nature are used as arenas within which one can listen, not halls of confusion or ignorance. More and more nature becomes the resource for the potential rejuvenation of humankind.

It is important to understand Merwin's attitude toward the living world so that we do not misinterpret his employment of silence in the nature poetry. Although Merwin is a poet of repetitive imagery and language, the meanings he places upon these are not static. The silence he evokes in his despair over history in *The Lice* is not the same as the natural silence in *The Compass Flower*. Thomas Byers points out that *The Lice* is a poetry de-signed in order to highlight irremediable differences between signifier and signified.[6] Following volumes, however, begin to find sustenance in the silences of nature. Getting out of the spoken, out of the written word is an avenue by which the poet may sift away the superfluous. Silence, therefore, should not be viewed in his naturism as evidence of futility, but, rather, as a tool of learning.

Michel Foucault professed the idea in *Les mots et les choses* that literature in the nineteenth century changed from a form of signification to a singular recognition of its own shaky existence and that this happening parallels the fall of the word at Babel. Basing his argument on Foucault's idea, Gerald L. Bruns defines modern poetry in general as an attempt to reexperience that fall. In the original world, before Babel, language was truly symbolic of the things it designated:

> It is perhaps impossible to speak of language without at some point invoking the myth of a primordial sign, which is to say the myth of an ideal unity of word and being. And in turn it is perhaps impossible to speak of this myth without taking up sooner or later the story of Babel, which duplicates typologically the story of man's fall from the harmony of his original paradise by dramatizing the fall of the word from its original harmony with the world. The story of Babel, after all, is not simply the story of the proliferation of tongues, but of the proliferation of words and their disproportionate abundance in relation to the world of things. The fall of the word, that is to say, is its dissociation from the world and its isolation among other words in "a space left vacant" by the world's disappearance.[7]

Bruns adds that for Martin Heidegger this negative discourse of poetry hides a "wealth of meanings" and that our job as readers is not to interpret, but, as Merwin also believes, to listen.[8] The *via negativa*, or route of absence, that critics so commonly observe in Merwin is the necessary forerunner of meaning in a world where traditional meanings have been destroyed by division, or the fall, from Eden or at Babel.

Often Merwin will depict silence as a cover that hides the value lying within nature. In character it is not so much an obstacle as a preliminary to a revelation that is uncertain yet, as in "The Well," happens periodically. "The Well" describes a voice that waits silently within water as certain living things try to draw upon it. In the poem the water expressed its voice when it embodied original unity, and it is apparent that the water will regain that unity because it will voice itself in the future: "Under the stone sky the water / waits / with all its songs inside it / the immortal / it sang once / it will sing again."[9] "Echoes" and "travellers" come to the water for its knowledge, but, as in all of Merwin's poetry, that which contains the genuine, in this case the voice, will express itself only when it is ready. That the water answers in "echoes" is demonstrative of the fall; the moment of restoration is not at hand. It appears that those who wait upon the voice will have to have patience for that which is pure mystery:

> Echoes come in like swallows
> calling to it
> it answers without moving
> but in echoes
> not in its voice
> . . . . . .
> It is a city to which many travellers
> came with clear minds
> having left everything even
> heaven
> to sit in the dark praying as one silence
> for the resurrection[10]

Those who wait upon the "resurrection" of the voice also must take on the quality of silence, for in understanding that such knowledge exists they understand that it will come quietly. They also have rejected more convenient offers of "heaven" from those who purport to have it. Such a belief in understanding through a silent awareness strongly resembles Buddhist beliefs, in which Merwin has long had an interest. Yet, Merwin was quick to point out in one interview that such influences should not be taken too specifically, by assuming that the poetry is representative of the entire philosophy.[11]

As well as in Buddhism, the value of silence is stressed in monastic groups with which Merwin had contact while traveling through Europe. In describing his visit to the monasteries on the mountain of Athos in his essay "Aspects of a Mountain," Merwin explains the practice of silence for the Greek Orthodox monks as exhibited by one abbot:

The abbot had received his own training, and had been instructed in the sacred teachings, by an elder, named Joseph, a holy man secluded somewhere on Athos, who had spent his life trying to rediscover the true hesychast (Hesychasts, "the Silent," from the Greek *hesychia*, "silence") tradition, of immeasurable age but certainly going back as far as the Desert Fathers, in the fourth century. The practice of hesychasm had involved, from the beginning, a constant inward awareness and invocation of God, a fervent meditative discipline of thoughts, and a corresponding struggle with distraction. It was, and it is, both a way of living and a state of being: it centers on a form of continual inner prayer, the prayer of the heart. Silence, ascetisicm, self-emptying, all directed toward a more intense focusing: at the dawn of the monastic age the Abbot Bessarion, in the desert, as he was dying, had said, "the monk should become, like the cherubim and seraphim, nothing but an eye."[12]

Thus, we see that there are possible religious influences for the closing off of speech in Merwin. However, as in his comment on Buddhism, the poetry is not bound with the whole religion, simply with this particular concept.

Like "The Well," the poem "Mist" offers silence as a mask for the genuine and a perspective from which to understand it better. "Mist" speaks of "tongues" that are "hiding in the trees," a mystical presence unseen and unheard: "their voices are hanging beyond the mist / seventy long banners mingling / red yellow / blue voices / hanging silent."[13]

To assert the existence of something he cannot sense, the speaker must simply rely upon his inclinations in the same way that the nuthatch leads the "white wind," which is invisible, through a world forested with "black trees" of absence: "here the nuthatch blows his horn / leading a thin procession of white wind // past the black trees / through the world."[14] By assigning the voices in the trees colors, the speaker is able to imagine them, but only visually—he offers no imaginative description of what they would sound like if they should express themselves. This technique blocks our auditory expectations as readers—yet the silence ultimately works as a nonrestrictive force. Protected in the "mist," the voices affirm their reality through the belief of the narrator. By closing the poem with the nuthatch's boldness to lead the "white wind," the narrator implies his kinship with the bird in their faith in the felt but intangible.

In "The Clear Skies" (from the same volume and which we examined in the disembodiment chapter), clouds actively try to communicate with modern-day humankind, but humankind has lost its original self and cannot gather either the courage or willingness to attempt restoration. With "Mist," Merwin bridges that gap, by allowing the narrator belief in nature's cognizant sounds.

In his review of *Writings to an Unfinished Accompaniment*, Laurence Lieberman comments upon the silences, compact language, and "bridges" between them, characterizing poems like "Mist" since Merwin's stylistic shift. Lieberman views this quality as indicative of a meaning that directs the reader toward it:

> To a degree surpassing every other poet of my acquaintance, writing in English or whatever language, W. S. Merwin has developed with increasing mastery in his last four volumes of verse a Matisse-like notation, a fantastic linguistic shorthand, in which the few irreducible lines and images chosen (or has he mastered, rather, the power of perfect submission, passivity, in allowing the inevitable lines and images to choose *him*, the translator's genius?) guide the reader's ear by unerringly exact bridges across the very hinges—invisible overlaps and interlockings—between the words to the silences behind, or surrounding, the spoken utterances. This wizardry is accomplished by chains of sound and echoes, the echoes of echoes, the tones and overtones—all matings that tie or bind sound to silence, tongue to its dumbness, voice to its muteness; and always, in Merwin's art at its best, that which is given, or revealed nakedly, releases by invisible art those quantities which are withheld, buried, concealed, but *contained* in the silence, and, therefore, inescapably picked up by the reader's ear, and poignantly heard, leading the reader into the heart of a vision of quietly gathering intensity, balanced halfway between sound and silence.[15]

Note Lieberman's focus on "chains of sound and echoes" as the instrument by which Merwin ties the spoken to the unspoken. Such a chain is created in "Mist" with the repetition of "hanging" and "voices," along with the alliteration of "white wind" and the assonance of "past the black trees" and "a thin procession of white wind." This echoing within the poem creates a sort of internal music, yet it is not the organicism of a perfectly self-contained work of art but that which directs the reader to consider what is intimated rather than spoken by the language. The poem resonates, but not simply within itself, for the imagery is too unusual. The camouflaging of the voices as colors stands as the perfect example of Merwin's refusal to speak that which cannot be spoken.

From an historical viewpoint, we may say that Merwin's poetry beginning with *Carrier* portrays the desire to have faith in the pre-neoclassical connection between knowledge and sign. As a poet of a modern age that according to Foucault is two philosophical removes from a belief in a preordained divine meaning, Merwin is uneasy to confirm such a relationship. However, Foucault's explanation of the Renaissance belief that "signs were thought to have been placed upon things so that men might be able to uncover their secrets, their natures

or their virtues" and that signs "did not need to be known in order
to exist: even if they remained silent, even if no one were to perceive
them, they were just as much *there*" represents the position that Merwin wishes to but cannot espouse.[16] His notions of the mysterious
remain much more skeptical than those of the Christian Renaissance
thinker, yet they have the important common attributes of inexplica-
bility, universality, and seeming benificence. Merwin is a poet of the
modern age for whom a fall has occurred. Signs may not relate to
any meaning, or they may be misread. There are, however, moments for
this poet when presence if not confirmed is at least deemed possible.

Typical of *The Moving Target* and *The Lice*, the two volumes immediately preceding *Carrier*, is the silence that designates absence. The poet
facing a disjointed world stands mute, like the day itself: "The day
hanging by its feet with a hole / In its voice / And the light running
into the sand // Here I am once again with my dry mouth / At the
fountain of thistles / Preparing to sing."[17]

In another poem, the voicelessness of creatures is symptomatic of
a world chaotic from its beginning to the present time: "And once
more I remember that the beginning // Is broken // No wonder
the addresses are torn // To which I make my way eating the silence
of animals / Offering snow to the darkness // Today belongs to few
and tomorrow to no one."[18] In a former pastoral landscape the silence
corresponds to a deathlike setting: "A silence before this one / Has
left its broken huts facing the pastures."[19]

With Merwin, however, habits are almost never without exception.
Interestingly, the despairing poet of *The Moving Target* chooses to close
that volume with ambiguity, if not potential, in "Daybreak," which
literally recedes to silence:

> Again this procession of the speechless
> Bringing me their words
> The future woke me with its silence
> I join the procession
> An open doorway
> Speaks for me
> Again[20]

The open doorway could designate a chance, or it could designate a
void. It would, however, be several years later and after a tenure on a
farm in France before Merwin's poetry could exhibit an unmistakable
presence of meaning through nature.[21]

When, with *Carrier*, this change appears, silence often assumes a completely contrary value to that in earlier volumes. A prayer to the ash tree in "In the Time of the Blossoms" voices hope for an "unbreathed music": "all over you leaf skeletons / fine as sparrow bones / stream out motionless / on white heaven / staves of one / unbreathed music / Sing to me."[22] Meditations such as "Silence / is my shepherd / Born once / born forever" and "Silent rivers / fall toward us / without explaining" no longer contain the hollow notes of modern humanity left with no comfort.[23]

Instead, the poet looks toward silence to lead him; it holds something he needs. In "The Piper," the narrator recognizes his inability to voice certain things: "it has taken me this long / to know what I cannot say / where it begins," but he also recognizes that the now inexpressible can clear a psychic space for wisdom: "Beginning / I am here / please / be ready to teach me / I am almost ready to learn."[24] *Carrier* is the first volume in which we observe the poet reaching out, in some cases as if he had entered the world anew. Epistemological openness becomes a trait in many poems, and it is doubtful that for Merwin this would have happened without his sense of restoration through nature.

Part of the task of openness involves giving up old ways of thinking. The purely logical program that people have been taught in order to become modern beings is clearly insufficient. "To the Rain" shows us that the human must learn to love that which is not available to the senses; empirical reasoning must be overcome. "Finding a Teacher" reiterates the same theme, within the specific field of silence. Learning through release, through a dispensing of the ego, formed a century and a half earlier a cornerstone of Keats's poetic philosophy. David Pollard explains that, for Keats, the poet in the "moodlessness of nonidentity" is able to imagine, and in this state it is silence that grants existence to things. The renunciation of identity in Keats, which we have discussed for Merwin in the disembodiment chapter, coexists with the renunciation of language, because, in the words of Keats, "'that which is creative must create itself.'"[25]

"Finding a Teacher" presents a narrator in the guise of a student, someone who expects to learn from a mentor figure, but who ends by having faith in the same mysterious natural forces that the teacher does. The speaker/student comes across "an old friend" fishing and begins to ask him about the universe and his own nature: "it was a question about the sun // about my two eyes / my ears my mouth /

my heart the earth with its four seasons / my feet where I was standing / where I was going."[26] However, the question, the rational attempt at grasping that which cannot be explained in logical categories, fails him, as do all attempts at such reduction. Merwin's common use of surrealism in his poetry and prose poems reveals his desire to debunk traditional categories of thinking that he sees as confining and ultimately deceptive. Surrealism underscores the narrator's abandonment of the easy answer:

> it slipped through my hands
> as though it were water
> into the river
> it flowed under the trees
> it sank under hulls far away[27]

Merwin will not end the poem with any ultimate sense of knowledge gained, mystical or otherwise. He will leave us, as he almost always does, with only the sense that something has been understood without language. This is all the narrator can hope for in a situation where truths will not be delivered outright, as the teacher in the poem well knows: "I no longer knew what to ask / I could tell that his line had no hook / I understood that I was to stay and eat with him."[28]

Language's inability to give us the answers that we wish to receive is a result of its separation from the natural order and a reflection of the futility of positivistic thinking. Modern language has suffered the effects of a history determined to divide it from reference to the natural world except through what has been permitted by science. If the thought we value will not allow the influence of the irrational or the mysterious, then language reflects that prejudice. To get out of language, to allow experience to influence consciousness and subconsciousness without the written or spoken word, is thus a necessary step for the poet if he is to understand anything beyond the surface of reality. By closing the poem with the upcoming meal to be shared between the teacher and the student, Merwin indicates that spiritual nourishment is available; it is simply not available by the means the student had expected.

Though Merwin uses brevity and white spaces along with the actual addressing of silence more than any other poet of his generation, there are a few others of this group to whom silence is also important. In particular, the "deep image" school with which Merwin is associated—which includes Robert Bly, Galway Kinnell, Mark Strand, and

James Wright—makes regular use of this in their emphasis upon the "deep" resonances of images that are available without literal exposition. In *The Branch Will Not Break*, James Wright depicts the silence that is needed for understanding to come:

> The moon drops one or two feathers into the field.
> The dark wheat listens.
> Be still.
> Now.
> There they are, the moon's young, trying
> Their wings.
> Between trees, a slender woman lifts up the lovely shadow
> Of her face, and now she steps into the air, now she is gone
> Wholly, into the air.[29]

Everything within this half of the poem, both in form and content, works toward the stillness and silence of a mystical atmosphere. The images are natural, even primal—the moon, dark wheat, a woman—and the focus upon these few elements in conjunction with the directive to "Be still," which seems to imply listening in the same manner as the wheat, invokes silence and mystery even before the woman disappears.

The admonition to silence (at least the narrator's admonition to himself if we do not read the third line as pertaining to the reader) is followed with listening to the quiet voices of this setting:

> I stand alone by an elder tree, I do not dare breathe
> Or move.
> I listen.
> The wheat leans back toward its own darkness,
> And I lean toward mine.[30]

The poem closes with a recognition of nature and the self. This work has more of an individual's self-exploration about it than those of Merwin's, yet it still is not a celebration of the particular ego. It is simultaneously about this poet's connections and recognized separation from the natural world, and it is about the value of meditation within silent spaces.

Robert Bly does not call upon silence as much in his poetry as Merwin, yet the situation into which he places his speakers is nevertheless that of the individual alone in nature with the few sounds of the world around him. In fact, the speaker of "Hunting Pheasants in a Cornfield" is as alone as a willow tree that he comes upon: "It is a willow tree alone in acres of dry corn. / Its leaves are scattered around its trunk, and around me, / Brown now, and speckled with delicate black, / Only the cornstalks now can make a noise."[31] The solitary images of the sun, some frozen weeds, and the branches of the tree mirror the concentration of Merwin and Wright. Like the narrators of Merwin, Bly's must stand alone in the silent spaces with only the surrounding natural scene.

Particularly interesting here is Bly's use of the word "body," which appears to refer to both tree and speaker: "The body is strangely torn, and cannot leave it. / At last I sit down beneath it."[32] By stepping into the life of the tree, the speaker steps into the world of nature, and the damaged condition, the "torn" body, of tree and speaker are repaired through their meeting. The single remaining sound is that of the wind blowing through the cornstalks, and the narrator imagines that if he were "a young animal," the tree would await him at dusk like a "home."[33] He professes, "I am happy in this ancient place," echoing Merwin's search for the original.[34]

One poem, "Kin," states that "at the end / birds lead something down to me / it is silence"—a stanza that says much about this important Merwin concept.[35] By employing silence in his poetry and by calling upon it, the poet extols a philosophy that is essentially at odds with the tradition of Western logic, but that has much in common with certain religious thought.

R. P. Blackmur, a key figure in New Criticism and a teacher and mentor of Merwin while he was at Princeton, defines silence in a 1955 essay in *The Sewanee Review* in much the same way as Heidegger does. By its very nature, silence stirs us to the meaning within:

> That is why we blush; it is in the blush that ripeness is all, and it is under the blush, in the honey of its generation, that we know the rest is silence. It is silence that tries to speak, and it is the language of silence which we translate into our words. If we do not hear the silence in our spoken or written words—if we do not hear their voice—we find them dead or vain echo calling on something already disappeared. If we do hear the silence we know that the words are animated by and united with a life not altogether their own, and superior to it; and with the same life we respond; we blush to a blush.[36]

Like disembodiment, the mystical path of silence for Merwin is a way toward understanding a mysterious existence that will not reveal itself openly. The poet has taken the despair-laden absences that once permeated his books and transformed them into opportunities for biotic initiation. Not all is silence in Merwin's geography, however. The original languages that once reflected the deep interconnection between indigenous peoples and nature, and that still exist in part, offer another opportunity for listening in the natural context.

Language and Nature

CORRESPONDING TO MERWIN'S SENSE THAT HUMANS ARE LIVING MORE AND more separately from the natural world is his belief that as time progresses cultures are also losing their historical ties between language and the planet. We have seen that language may be used as a device that divides humans from the natural world by establishing a system of codes and an epistemology that exalts humanity at the expense of other living things and that this is a primary reason for Merwin's use of silence. However, cultures, especially native cultures, have traditionally had words and phrases in their language binding their everyday lives to their particular natural environment. As the physical world becomes increasingly removed from the lives of these peoples, however, so the language that they have used to refer to their surroundings has been disappearing.

The depletion of our ability to adequately refer to our world (and to ourselves) may also be observed in nonnative societies. Merwin believes that language is not something dissociated from the rest of people's existence, that it is not an arbitrary system with elements equally exchangeable with any others, but that it is an indicator of our condition as a society. In an interview published in 1982, he spoke of the relationship between ourselves and our speech in the present-day:

> Well, I think that what we perceive in the language around us, what our language is telling us, is something about the quality of our own existence. It is telling us at the moment that the quality of our existence as a species, as a time, a moment in geologic and astronomic and historic time, is in great, great danger. It's in terrible jeopardy. We have all kinds of theoretical and perceptual responses to that, but I think the language itself is in bad shape at the moment.[1]

Merwin continued by comparing this event to ecological damage: "If our use of the language ... is imprecise and cheap and shabby, then there's a kind of pollution creeping into our lives."[2] The debasing of speech and writing through the careless use of it and its exploitation by politicians and the media are a gauge of the condition of our culture. Noting that speech is no longer being used as it was by the nomads and hunters of the past, "whose entire life was inside every word," Robert Bly remarks on the same phenomenon: "Now you have language being used by professional liars, who are also called advertising men, and men who are not interested in the meaning of the word;..."[3] The damage to language, simultaneous with our schism from nature, presents a tragic scenario for poets concerned with both. Merwin's ideas about the connection between the natural world and language may be seen in the following passage, where he freely moved to speaking of the environment while answering a question about the Hawaiian tongue:

> It's very hard to hear Hawaiian. We—white Anglo-Saxons and subsequent waves of people who have been imported to get the economy rolling, to get large scale agriculture on its feet—we have done terrible things to that culture. We have all but destroyed it. It's very hard to hear Hawaiian spoken, which I think goes along with ecological damage to the islands, which is simply immeasurable.[4]

The Rain in the Trees, Merwin's 1988 volume, contains numerous poems that treat the language/nature breakdown. "At the Same Time," which appears roughly mid-volume, sets the stage for the following poems on the topic. "At the Same Time" begins with a pointed exposé of the shallow epistemology of modern Western culture—that it is only our contemporaries from whom we try to learn, with whom we communicate. We do not make attempts to learn from those of the past, "for the dead do not listen to us."[5] Such a gesture would require modern humanity's putting aside the belief in its superiority to listen to the stories of past cultures. Similarly, we think that we have nothing to say to future generations that will discover what we will leave behind because they will be unable to understand the world as we now perceive it. Our particular perspective of the landscape will have passed on, so what is there to tell? The narrator asks what good it would do humankind to be discovered a century later, because "this sky" will have changed and "these valleys" will be "unknown."[6]

This historical isolation, this self-imposed, self-serving parochialism, is betrayed in language. Evidence of our attitudes lies in the way we have relegated ourselves to "addresses" that connect us to place in a temporary manner.[7] All we are left with, or, more properly, leave ourselves with, is the sound of our own voices. We refuse to link ourselves to others who have lived or will live "where we are talking and writing."[8] This relativism, which is in part found in the lack of a language to bind us to a more permanent planet, is symptomatic of a culture that cares for little outside of itself. Our society-centered and species-centered rhetoric indicates that we are perceptually fixed in one time within our own kind. Additionally, this one time has as its icons materialism and immediate pleasure. Little concern for the future of the earth or the lessons of past cultures enters the lives of the poet's contemporary citizens of a society characterized by self-erasure. As we have migrated, we have taken our cultural chauvinism with us and imposed it upon those with whom we have come into contact.

Since the mid-seventies Merwin has lived in Hawaii, and from his conversations with Native Hawaiians he has learned of their multifaceted loss, which he, in turn, presents from the native perspective in one poem. The poem depicts the historically rapid change in their culture and the fact that many Hawaiians have witnessed expressions that psychologically situated them in their environment fall out of usage. "Losing a Language" is narrated by a Native Hawaiian who is too young to know the traditional language but who tells us that the old still remember some of the place-oriented speech. All that he can offer and comprehend is a translation of its meaning because he is spiritually and culturally cut off from the world that created it and used it:

> A breath leaves the sentences and does not come back
> yet the old still remember something that they could say
>
> but they know now that such things are no longer believed
> and the young have fewer words
>
> many of the things the words were about
> no longer exist
>
> the noun for standing in mist by a haunted tree
> the verb for I[9]

With the solidifying of the newcomers' culture among the natives, the young will not learn the phrases of their parents and grandparents and are told that they should entirely adopt the new culture. Typically, the conquerors perceive the natives as inferior, and, standing ethnically apart from the new society, the narrator expresses his alienation from it: "where nothing that is here is known / we have little to say to each other // we are wrong and dark / in the eyes of the new owners // the radio is incomprehensible / the day is glass // when there is a voice at the door it is foreign / everywhere instead of a name there is a lie."[10]

Because of the degradation of language, the people "have little to say to each other," and instead of having truly referential names for the things in their lives, the language is filled with distortions. The progress of this loss historically is rapid, but within the lives of a group of people it is so subtle that "nobody has seen it happening" and "nobody remembers."[11] All that the narrator can summon of the lost language is a remembrance of its past powers to predict such tragedy: "this is what the words were made / to prophesy // here are the extinct feathers / here is the rain we saw."[12]

In Merwin's mythography, the language of nature serves as the logos, the eternal word synonymous with meaning. The obliteration of the logos is part of the destruction of native cultures through assimilation, which, consequently, has its implications for the natural world, because identification with the planet is necessary for its preservation.

When commenting upon Merwin, critics have often summoned Thoreau, but rarely Roethke. Strong similarities do exist between the two, however, and these lie within the language/nature equation. In a 1950 essay entitled "The Vegetal Radicalism of Theodore Roethke," Kenneth Burke examines the language of nature toward which Roethke strives. For what he terms "three strategic moments in the theory of poetic selectivity" as comparison, Burke cites Dante Alighieri, Wordsworth, and D. H. Lawrence. Burke observes: " . . . we can see in Roethke's cult of 'intuitive' language: a more strictly 'infantile' variant of the Dantesque search for a 'noble' vernacular; a somewhat suburban, horticulturalist variant of Wordsworth's stress upon the universal nature of rusticity; and a close replica of Lawrence's distinction between the 'physical' and the 'abstract.'"[13] By synopsizing these important thematic and stylistic strains in Roethke, Burke encapsulates what in this poet is analogous and what is not analogous to Merwin.

Roethke's "infantile" speech—his common use of childish language, gibberish, and nursery rhymes—for the most part is not found in

Merwin. A very few Merwin poems consciously imitate children's lyric, but these are rare. Their point of convergence is where Roethke allows himself extended contemplation of the natural world, the Roethke of "Meditation at Oyster River," "The Far Field," and "Journey to the Interior."

Concerning the "infantile," Roethke's search for the father has often been discussed, and some psychoanalytic theory generalizes all desire for nature as regressive, as a movement backward toward a primal mother. Rosemary Sullivan points out that in his early career Jung associated the "mystic impulse" (which we may correspond to Merwin's drive toward natural mystery) with a desire to reestablish the joy of the ouroboros but that Jung later denounced this theory, believing the impulse to be a fundamental part of human psychology.[14] Moreover, the push toward the unconscious, the irrational, or the primal has often in Eastern religion and native cultures been a path of spiritual and intellectual growth.

Burke's points about rusticity and the physical are where we find the two poets' strongest commonality, and these concepts also help illuminate our understanding of the language of nature in Merwin. Roethke's rusticity is, as Burke points out, rather "horticulturalist," but it is wild too. The language denoting nature, the imagery—the currents, moons, and flowers—comprises most of Roethke's poetry and much of Merwin's as well. Nature is expressed most often in the "physical," a hard vocabulary that also dominates Merwin's vernacular. We should be quick to add, however, that for Merwin this "physical" speech is also represented extensively in nonnatural elements like "keys," "doors," and "locks" in several books of the sixties and early seventies. In contrast to the twisting abstractions and plays upon logic in his earliest volumes, the physical and "rustic" become by mid-career the vocabulary of reality that grounds his later poetry.

Seeking the physical and rustic, several poems from *The Rain in the Trees* express a desire on the part of the narrators to speak the natural tongue despite the fact that they sense the difficulty of doing so—"Hearing the Names of the Valleys," "Tracing the Letters," "Witness," and "After the Alphabets." In "Hearing the Names of the Valleys," the language of nature is not native to the speaker; he is culturally and historically divided from the logos of his environs. The poem is delivered from the point of view of an outsider, but an outsider, like Merwin, who is sympathetic to the loss of holistic living and the natural world. Describing a conversation between a newcomer and an old native, the speaker tries to learn some of the original language but finds himself unable to.

The referential tongue of the natives even includes naming the water that flows from particular rocks. Binding word to thing, each place has unique meaning. The lesson for the speaker is one of his cultural poverty:

> for a long time I asked him the names
> and when he says them at last
> I hear no meaning
> and cannot remember the sounds
>
> I have lived without knowing
> the names for the water
> from one rock
> and the water from another
> and behind the names that I do not have
> the color of water flows all day and all night[15]

As soon as the old man tells him the traditional name for the water, he forgets it. Having existed in a culture apart from nature, the narrator discovers that the original is not so easy to acquire. Implicit in the poem is not simply the idea that learning a language is difficult, but that establishing the connections to nature that have been lost through history may be impossible. Instead of traveling from rock to rock, the water now moves by means of plumbing, and the overall loss, of nature and language, is tantamount to death: "there are names for the water / between here and there / ... except in the porcelain faces / on the tombstones."[16]

The poem ends with the speaker still hoping that he will be able to revive some of the lost language, and, as in the poems of origin, the notion of "remembering" appears: "and I ask him again / the name for the color of water / wanting to be able to say it / as though I had known it all my life / without giving it a thought."[17]

Although Merwin does not believe that we can locate any point in history when the damage to the natural world began, we can point to the eighteenth century and its scientific movements as embodying a certain objectification of nature. Merwin's 1991 essay, "The Tree on One Tree Hill," describes the explorations of Captain Cook and his crew to the Pacific in the latter half of the eighteenth century and their subsequent introduction of the newest and most scientific methods of schematizing nature. The methods of classifying life, which the

naturalists on Cook's ship the *Endeavor* employed, corresponded to
the desire of ownership, the colonial aspiration that was the reason
for their voyage. In the following passage, Merwin describes the naturalists' new methods, referring also to "developments" in navigational
instruments and maps that made explorations more sure, as well as the
ostensible reason for the expedition—the observation of the Transit of
Venus from the antipodes. On board one circumnavigation of the
earth on the *Endeavor* was artist Sydney Parkinson, whose job was to
paint new species as he found them:[18]

> The Linnaean system for classifying and naming the natural world was
> an analogous development, a product of the same urge and the same
> moment—the moment that Sydney Parkinson was painting. He was ob-
> serving another Transit, in fact, except that the light that disappeared
> behind the new system of knowledge would not emerge again. The world
> that the Europeans "discovered" began to vanish as they set eyes on it,
> and to decompose at their touch. Their words for what they wanted from
> it even as observers are telling: they must "seize it," "capture it" once and
> for all, to "take home"—for home was somewhere else, somewhere already
> known and intrinsically different.[19]

Merwin goes on in the essay to explain that the system of describing
nature that Linnaeus developed often indicated the organism's place
within that biological hierarchy, and, often, the names of the naturalists
examining the species or the patrons of the expedition. He says, "such
a view, . . . tends sometimes to assume that a perfect and accessible
truth can exist in separation from life itself, which is never finished,
never in that sense perfect, . . ."[20]

In contrast to the Linnaean system that scientists embraced at the
time, Merwin tells us of a German-born naturalist, Georg Everard
Rump, later known as Rumphius, who had come to the islands of the
South Pacific more than 100 years before Cook and who had a different
way of looking at nature. Rumphius's education would probably have
included the Roman naturalist Pliny as well as Aristotle, and in his
more than 700 chapter *Herbal* of the island of Ambon in twelve books
and in his thesaurus of sea creatures and minerals he did originally
write in Latin. However, as Merwin explains, Rumphius also wrote
in a way that the naturalists on the *Endeavor* would not have deemed
appropriate. He often described plants and animals in the language
of an ordinary person witnessing them as living beings, a method that
would return in the nineteenth century as it was beginning to be

known that nature was endangered by humans. Rumphius also rewrote his *Herbal* in Dutch, which had become his everyday speech, and in this translation he shows that he is a part of the world he is perceiving, that he is psychologically bound to it.[21] To demonstrate the closeness of this observer and his world, Merwin chooses a passage about hermit crabs (which live in the shells of other animals) absconding with the shells of some whelks Rumphius had left out. The passage is from an English translation of the rewritten *Herbal*, of which I shall quote a part:

> These little quarrelsome creatures have caused me much grief, because when I laid out all kinds of handsome whelks to bleach, even on a high bank, they knew how to climb up there at night, and carried the beautiful shells with them, leaving me their old coats to peep at.[22]

Despite his personal and interactive portraits—the difference from those who would follow him—Rumphius described what he saw in the languages of Europe and approached the South Pacific with a Western attitude, as he necessarily had to.[23] Merwin's poem celebrating this naturalist, "The Blind Seer of Ambon," is narrated by the subject himself, and in the poem Rumphius recognizes his otherness to the environment and the way of seeing he has brought with him from his culture.

Rumphius suffered numerous tragedies in his life, including the loss of his wife and daughter in an earthquake, the loss of several manuscripts in fire or at sea, and the loss of his vision. The living things that he studies, however, the things that embody "no value that we know," give him sustenance to continue his life after these misfortunes.[24] By discovering the stories of the creatures, the importance of their lives, he ventures upon a continuous exploration that becomes his own salvation:

> so this is the way I see now
> I take a shell in my hand
> new to itself and to me
> I feel the thinness the warmth and the cold
>
> . . . .
>
> everything takes me by surprise
> it is all awake in the darkness[25]

The Rumphius portrayed by Merwin and by his own records allowed himself to be open to nature and sentient in response to it, like the narrators in the poems of origin. Although the naturalist was not from the islands in which he came to live most of his life, he, nevertheless, often approached that world very differently from those who had the more "sophisticated" methodology of 100 years later.

Up until now we have been discussing the language of nature in terms of how humans may represent their environment, how the planet may be signified by human speech. However, two poems from *The Rain in the Trees*, "Tracing the Letters" and "After the Alphabets," push the "language" of nature into its most primal sense. In these poems, nature itself voices a vernacular of meaning, and the speakers' desire is to travel forward to the time when they will understand this tongue resurrected from prehistory. In "Tracing the Letters" the sounds of the planet will be understood by the narrator when he will overcome division. This "green" language is constantly being recorded by the universe, and the text that the speaker will be able to understand will demonstrate the organic character of all things: "When I learn to read / I will know how green is spelled"; it is the "one word" that will survive, even if temporarily obscured.[26] In "After the Alphabets" the communication of the ancient and lowly insects becomes for the speaker the language of the postapocalyptic future, and the arcane meanings of this language hold the mysteries of the workings of the planet. The speaker begins by stating that he is trying to learn this future speech, which is quite different from that of humans:

> I am trying to decipher the language of insects
> they are the tongues of the future
> their vocabularies describe buildings as food
> they can depict dark water and the veins of trees
> they can convey what they do not know
> and what is known at a distance
> and what nobody knows[27]

Learning the insects' tongue means learning about the workings of life, and the vocabulary of "Tracing the Letters" will be available to its speaker along with an awakening of primal knowledge. The text that this speaker will "read" will be inscribed with the living reptilian imagery that recedes all the way back to origin. When he discovers "the stories" that contain "green" in their pages, he will become reacquainted with the "green hands," "eyelids," and "eyes" of the ancient.[28]

Particularly stressed in "After the Alphabets" is the idea that the natural text embraces holistic meaning. The insects not only act and communicate with the world in physical terms; they also trade the hieratic messages upon whose meaning life is founded. This communication is as perfect as can be imagined, and it voices the organicism necessary for all life: "they have terms for making music with the legs / . . . the speakers are their own meaning in a grammar without horizons / . . . they are never important they are everything."[29] If we were able to ascribe a geometric figure to represent these two poems, that figure would certainly be a circle. Time, ancient and future, coalesces, as does the value of the smallest and the largest.

Many of these poems dealing with humans' use of a "natural" language or the desire to interpret the meaning of nature may seem fantastical and unrelated to the world at hand. Yet, Merwin's belief is that personal links to nature are necessary to maintain a proper respect for it, which is, in turn, necessary for its survival. The industrial and technological impact upon nature that the people of "advanced" societies have inflicted upon it is evidence to support his belief. To give us a historical background for ecological destruction, he has written numerous poems retelling particular events and moments associated with alterations of landscapes and the ideological agendas that prepared them. These historical poems, which usually focus on the New World, nevertheless offer us a broad picture of how we have come to a worldwide moment of crisis.

6

New World Conquerors and the
Environmental Crisis

ONE OF W. S. MERWIN'S MAJOR TOPICS OVER THE YEARS IN BOTH POETRY AND prose has been the environmental crisis. Merwin's outspokenness on the subject began in his poetry with *The Lice* (1967) and appeared in scattered poems in later volumes until the publication of *The Rain in the Trees* (1988), where it stands as a dominant theme. Our present treatment of the environment in the West is aggravated by the concept of nature as an economic resource, by the history of an order-centered theology, and by a scientific viewpoint, beginning in the Renaissance and prevalent by the Enlightenment, which sees nature solely as an object of study. The alternative that Merwin finds is that of the native peoples of America and Hawaii, whose spiritual perspective of the living world embraces an ecological regard absent in Western societies.

The environment is to Merwin the most crucial issue facing human beings, one that can no longer be ignored. How we treat the world around us is a result of how we view it and how we view ourselves. Presently, as we lose our ties to the natural world and no longer even realize that we are losing them, the potential for abuse multiplies. A humankind dissociated from the natural world, that believes that it can find all of its answers within institutions and technology, will believe that these same entities can manage the earth also.

In various interviews, Merwin has said that he has little hope for humankind's future. Yet, his tireless addressing of the ecological situation indicates that he cannot resign himself to nihilism. In 1980 he said that his handling of his despair has changed since the sixties—when he was acutely feeling the problems of Vietnam and nuclear proliferation—yet the despair itself still remains with him:

> I don't feel any less pessimistic now, but my relation to the pessimism, I
> think, has changed. I don't feel as floored by it, and that's really something

unusual, because the things that made me feel pessimistic then are certainly still with us and more so: the destruction of the natural world, the really insane exploitation of the whole environment, the pollution of the elements, and an economy that's really based on war and greed—we just seem to be heading straight for complete physical destruction.[1]

Merwin's love for nature, as evident in his poems of an original world, makes him more aware than most writers, and most people, of the tenuous condition it exists in all over the planet. The same poet who rejoices when he discovers a glimpse of his place in the natural scheme of things and who writes to bring about such moments often feels angered by humankind's abuses. Merwin does not propose that such mistakes are new to humankind, yet he thinks that they appear now to be happening at an alarming rate.[2]

The ecological damage Merwin is concerned about is occurring all around the world and in certain areas has been noticeable for many centuries. Gary Snyder, another poet consistently vocal about the environment, reveals in *The Practice of the Wild* that most of China's lowland hardwood forests were gone by about 3,500 years ago and that in Japan the original deciduous hardwoods are found now only in the most isolated mountains.[3] The religious pasts of Japan and China, with Taoism, Buddhism, and Shintoism, have been rich in their respect for nature, but even the practitioners of these faiths have had to find refuge in the mountains where land cannot be used for agriculture or commerce.[4] Many of Merwin's poems address the ecological situation in general, implicitly, for wherever loss occurs. Yet, many others specifically question the policy, past and present, of the United States, and in these poems the poet seems to be saying that a national self-analysis is sorely needed.

In the Western Hemisphere, much of the damage to nature has been a product of the colonization and exploitation of the New World. If a people's attitude is that the land awaits conquering, that it is the destiny of humankind to "tame" wild areas (which includes the "civilization," banishment, or extermination of indigenous societies), then natural destruction will follow closely behind. Primarily, the poems that treat the history of environmental destruction have appeared in *The Carrier of Ladders* and *The Rain in the Trees*. In the first volume, Merwin's eye is upon the American mainland—in particular, westward expansion—whereas in the second he speaks of Hawaii, his present home. To look critically at Western native societies, we should note that these peoples have sometimes been responsible for their own incidents of ecological loss.

In *Killing the White Man's Indian*, Fergus M. Bordewich asserts that the Iroquois broke off the entire tops of trees in order to harvest cherries, and before the landing of Europeans they likely overhunted numerous large animals. Tribes, observes Bordewich, would often exhaust the natural resources of an area and then travel to another location. Also before the arrival of the white people, the Plains Indians, famous for their reverence of the buffalo, would harvest certain parts, leaving the rest to spoil.[5] Although it is extremely difficult to make quantifiable comparisons between preindustrial and industrial societies, societies from one area of the world with a specific set of resources and conditions with those from another area of the world, and societies with a particular population density with those of another density, it seems to me that Bordewich's evidence is somewhat valid and somewhat invalid. His suppositions involving the overhunting of large animals may be demographically reasonable, but they leave a considerable amount of uncertainty as to the degree of overhunting involved.[6] We are certain, however, that in Britain, bears, wolves, and beavers have all been eliminated for centuries as a consequence of sport, fear, or the desire for their fur. We also know, for example, that not long after America's settling, between 1750 and 1860, France had leveled no less than 50 percent of its forests, precipitating floods, soil erosion, and timber shortages.[7] Degradation of this kind was never witnessed by the Europeans who set foot on the continent inhabited by Indians. We also know that the damage in Merwin's Hawaii caused by indigenous farming pales in relation to the depletion from early plantation agriculture, to say nothing of the loss of human life by the incidental importation of smallpox.

It appears that the religious attitudes of indigenous peoples in America did contribute significantly to their environmental health. Some have criticized present-day Native Americans who affirm a history of ecological respect on the grounds that the Indians are "romanticizing" themselves, constructing a fabled self-image in an effort to salvage a destroyed past. These critics fail to listen when the Native Americans explain that their attitudes are abundantly present in their stories and myths. Their tales may reflect the literal, historical events of a tribe, or they may be windows into beliefs that sustain a transgenerational ecocentrism. Peter Matthiesen observes that to desecrate the planet would be, for the Indian, to desecrate the Creator.

Nor do the Indians "worship" nature, which requires a distance from it: "Man is an aspect of nature, and nature itself is a manifestation of primordial religion. . . . Nature is the 'Great Mysterious,' the 'religion before religion,' the profound intuitive apprehension of the true nature of existence attained by sages of all epochs, everywhere on earth . . ."[8]

By contrast, the colonists' spiritual paradigms shaped their perceptions of America in a very different way. Roy Harvey Pearce's *Savagism and Civilization* explains the early settlers' displacement of the Indians and their conflicts with them as the product of the imposition of European theology. It was not simply a newcomer's quest for land that marked the colonists, but also a religious philosophy that sanctioned dominion:

> The Renaissance Englishmen who became Americans were sustained by an idea of order. They were sure, above all, of the existence of an eternal and immutable principle which guaranteed the intelligibility of their relations to each other and to their world and thus made possible their life in society. It was a principle to be expressed in the progress and elevation of civilized men who, striving to imitate their God, would bring order to chaos. America was such a chaos, a new-found chaos. Her natural wealth was there for the taking because it was there for the ordering. So were her natural men. . . . And they knew that the way to civilize a world was to civilize the men in it.[9]

Notions of the Indian as barbaric and in need of civilization never disappeared, but by the mid-eighteenth century the Native American was more closely taking on the role of Noble Savage by the essayists of America. The Noble Savage stereotype, of course, may have idealized Indians but failed to present them as human beings with human needs and did little to protect their rights to the continent they depended upon for sustenance. Whatever the divergent ideas on the character of the original people, progress and order continued their onward push.[10] In the real experience of settling the country, European Americans continued to expel and isolate the Native American. Far from taking any lessons from native culture, Peter Nabokov remarks that whites bought, stole, fenced, tilled, and built upon the land "with an abandon that horrified Indians."[11]

Merwin's "The Gardens of Zuñi," from *The Carrier of Ladders,* has as its subject John Wesley Powell, the nineteenth-century geologist and ethnologist. Powell's endeavors ranged from plans for then-modernized systems of agriculture for the American West and explorations of the gorges of the Green and Colorado rivers to a study of Indian languages of the region. As one of the first to propose the reclamation of arid lands through the building of dams and irrigation projects, he has been traditionally hailed as a conservationist.[12] However, the utilization of the West for farming, mining, and lumbering has altered the land, very often to its detriment. Powell had argued against the inexhaustibility of natural resources, but despite this relative insight, his concept of large-scale reclamation of arid lands did not recognize that the desert *is* a working ecosystem. In Merwin's poem, Powell serves as a symbol of the country's westward expansion and our failure as a nation to question our actions. Interestingly, the explorer had lost one arm during the Civil War, a loss that parallelled our own as we conquered the wilderness:

> The one-armed explorer
> could touch only half of the country
>
> . . . .
> He is long dead with his five fingers
> and the sum of their touching
> and the memory
> of the other hand
> his scout
> . . . .
>
> while he balanced
> balanced
> and groped on
> for the virgin land
>
> and found where it had been[13]

Before the explorers, the Indians had managed to preserve the land; their fires gave "no more heat / than the stars" and did not entail the "bleeding" of intensive use of the land.[14] As the continent was beginning to be severed by exploration, the severed hand of Powell, "his scout," accompanies him only in "memory." The absence of the hand underscores the absence of a valid ethos in the westward push. Consequently, language becomes nullified in this situation; Merwin states that the missing hand can send back no message.

As Americans we were, and still are, determined to capture that which cannot be captured. The repeated balancing of Powell in the poem conveys the image of one who awkwardly makes his way ahead on a journey whose outcome he does not understand. Powell thus signifies not so much himself as the American program in the West—stumbling, incomplete, yet determined to discover and hold the wilderness, which disappears by those very actions. In contrast, the ways of the Native American offer a personal wholeness unattainable by possession: "this love of earth, this respectful awareness of the world around, of its warnings and its affirmations, brings a joyous humility, a *simplicity* that spares the Indian the great restlessness and loneliness that the alienated white men have brought down upon themselves."[15]

"The Gardens of Zuñi" actually belongs to an "American" sequence of poems, which runs from "The Approaches" through "The Removal" in *The Carrier of Ladders*.[16] "Western Country," "Other Travellers to the River," and "The Trail into Kansas" are other poems within this series that unmistakably focus on the settling of the American West; "Homeland," "The Free," "The Prints," and "The Removal" reenact the 1830s eviction of the Five Civilized Tribes from ancestral lands. Whereas "The Gardens of Zuñi" and "Other Travellers to the River" have explorers as subjects, "Western Country" treats the masses who moved westward. Their "faith" in moving is that people do not die in exile, a symptom of their belief that the land inherently calls to be settled—the Puritan concept of order that Roy Harvey Pearce describes. Yet, the narrator explains that the only truth is that "death is not exile."[17] Like the educated Powell in "The Gardens of Zuñi," these ordinary people also long for the untouched land: "Each no doubt knows a western country / half discovered / which he thinks is there because / he thinks he left it / and its names are still written in the sun / in his age and he knows them / but he will never tread their ground."[18] Spatial absolutes collapse as the injustices of the past crowd in upon the narrator; and the broad expanses, which once maintained the wild, diminish to the gap between trigger and finger: "At some distances I can no longer / sleep / my countrymen are more cruel than their stars / and I know what moves the long / files stretching into the mountains / each man with his gun / his feet / one finger's breadth off the ground."[19]

The dream of possession moves the files of people into the wilderness territory—that and the belief that it is their destiny. Implicit in the poem's handling of the 1830s Indian removal to the West is such naïveté. Andrew Jackson, similar to many settlers, embraced the justifiability of Indian expulsion and, subsequently, shifted his opinions into heinous momentum. As President, Jackson signed the Indian Removal Act, authorizing the mass forced relocation of Southeastern Indians to lands west of the Mississippi and later ignored a Supreme Court decision won by the Cherokees to halt the exodus. In "Homeland" the terrible act is signified by the sky containing "all the barbed wire of the west / in its veins," while the poet executes his own justice by having the sun drive a stake through the vampirelike "black heart of Andrew Jackson."[20]

To explain such strong sentiment on the poet's part, it should be observed that during the march, better known as the "Trail of Tears," thousands of Indians lost their lives. Shortages existed for almost all supplies, including food; disease was extensive; and the treatment of the Indians at the hands of the soldiers was often severe.[21] At the time of *Carrier*'s publication—1970—little had been said about this chapter in American history. Even earlier, however, the national attitude found in "Western Country," which ended the untamed land in the West, had spurred Merwin's interest in doing a project on it.

In 1959, Merwin officially began work on a long narrative poem about an 1894 march to Washington, D.C., by Jacob Coxey and his army of the unemployed. Merwin worked on the poem erratically over the next several years, and he even began tracing the path of the unemployed workers across Pennsylvania but never finished it.[22] The significance of Coxey's army to Merwin lies largely in its correspondence to the closing of the West. After all of the conquering had been done, the damage to humans was beginning to show as it had already begun to show with the environment. As Merwin relates the two events,

> There was no longer any West for a man to go to, not in the old sense. It ended. The buffalo had been killed off, the Indians had been rounded up, mostly—none of this destructive afflatus was going to work anymore; it wasn't the answer. Doing such things was an anachronism. And so we had the first petitioning groups walk on the White House lawn. This wasn't treated as anything of great importance, but I think it was a crucial moment.[23]

In several of his poems on Hawaii from *The Rain in the Trees*, the extinction of the native culture goes hand in hand with environmental destruction. Particularly frightening is the history of conquerors, who, having no concept of the characteristics of the area they have gone into, are able to change the culture of the original inhabitants.

Without a psychological connection to the land, the chance of maintaining a necessary respect for it is greatly diminished.

In *The Rain in the Trees*, Merwin's original Hawaiians embody ties to place as do the Indians in *Carrier*. The Hawaiians both do and do not accept the conquerers, who manage to take from the land whatever they wish. The entire process of ecological and cultural change in an area with a native people reads for Merwin as the history of a tragedy. "The Strangers from the Horizon" describes the start of the intrusion into Hawaii with the first European explorers, as told by one of the Hawaiians who witnessed it. Two ships arrive early one morning, evincing an enormity that, to the natives, is rivaled only by the natural world.

The power of the sailors leads the people of the island to welcome their coming; yet, the huge, black ships with "teeth along the sides" (which are probably cannons) and their "many arms" depict for us the character of the newcomers.[24] They are soldiers ready to fight. Their sails that seem like clouds and their ships' masts that are no longer trees distinguish them from the natives, who have not used nature on such a scale. The Hawaiians, however, are not naive as to the truth about the explorers—they are cognizant "that they [are] not gods."[25] The final lines of the poem portray the natives taking goods, which they ironically state are needed, out to the sailors. It is obvious that the sailors simply desire the items for profit or greed, and it is also certain that the natives comprehend the duplicity of their visitors.

The scene depicted is apparently based upon one of the landings of Captain Cook's *Resolution* and *Discovery* in Hawaii in 1778 and 1779. Although the Europeans' arrival is rather ominous, the natives in "The Strangers from the Horizon" welcome them because of the strength they outwardly manifest, a fact in all probability and one that Merwin does not gloss over. To accurately present Hawaiian society of the time, it is important to note that the leadership of the different islands was divided into four "kingdoms" with separate chiefs and that wars among the Hawaiians were frequent and bloody. In Merwin's poem, the people never believe that the sailors are gods. Historically, upon Cook's landing on both occasions, excitement was high-pitched among the people that the god Lono had returned with his companion-gods, and it was not until the avarice of the explorers was suffered that fatal tensions broke out between Cook's men and the natives.[26] Merwin's omission (if we may call it that) may have been made in order to avoid the theatrical and to stress the Europeans' motivation. Rightfully, "The Strangers from the Horizon" objects to the arrogance and vices of the outsiders and foreshadows the string of adversities that were to come with immigration and colonization.

This final phase—colonization—and the native attitude concerning it follow in "Conqueror," a companion poem to "The Strangers from the Horizon." This poem, spoken by an omniscient narrator in a questioning mode that Merwin frequently employs, reveals that the Hawaiians may not be so happy with the coming of the explorers. The poem works through the outward extinction of a culture yet leaves open to debate the possibility of changing a people's entire way of viewing the world:

> When they start to wear your clothes
> do their dreams become more like yours
> who do they look like
>
> when they start to use your language
> do they say what you say
> who are they in your words
>
> when they start to use your money
> do they need the same things you need[27]

The conquerors, who see things only in terms of externalities, cannot comprehend that the Hawaiians may or may not be able to conform to their ways. To the conquerors, introducing their clothes, language, and money to a people means winning them as much as winning their land. However, complete subversion may not be so easy. As it is not discernible to whom the people pray after they have supposedly been converted over to new gods, what they pray might also surprise the outsiders: "when they are converted to your gods / do you know who they are praying to / do you know who is praying // for you not to be there."[28] With this twist, Merwin recreates the Prospero-Caliban motif. The slave, or the conquered, who has been taught his master's language, uses that very language to curse him. In the best scenarios, the original inhabitants maintain a sense of place and have not been brainwashed into accepting another culture's way of thinking, even if they have assimilated its lifestyle. All too often, however, when many of the outward signs of the original culture are lost and the colonists establish their lives among the original inhabitants, then ways of thinking change too.

The Hawaiians' traditional kinship with nature is represented by

Merwin in several poems. The cultural and religious ties between the Hawaiian and the natural world are numerous, and it is, therefore, impossible to speak of a traditional Hawaiian society without discussing nature. Michael Kioni Dudley describes their "familial belonging" to a conscious world:

> To summarize the ways one might be related to nature, then, one might be related as family through direct evolutionary descent, as the *Kumulipo* [a genealogical chant] showed all humans were. If one could trace direct descent in his genealogy from one of the high gods, he would be further related to all of the *kino lau* [multiple forms] which that god assumed. If one were descended from a god who ordinarily dwelt in a nature-form but who had taken human-form to mate with a woman, the descendant would be related to the nature form of his ancestor. If one had an ancestor who at death had assumed some natural form—either like a chief going into a star, or like a person deified through *kākū'ai* being assumed into a shark god or some other form of nature—that person was also related to the nature form of that ancestor. Because of his belief in *kino lau*, the Hawaiian who today practices the traditional religion, when looking at a mountain, feels his relationship to his god Kū in that mountain form. Looking at the sun, he views a presence of his god, Kāne, and experiences the god's warmth on his body.... Nature is not only conscious, much of it is divine. And as he interrelates with and interacts with nature, he interrelates and interacts with the gods.[29]

We can easily see from this brief account of Hawaiian belief the radical differences in attitudes about nature between Native Hawaiians and Europeans. The intermingling of the natural and the spiritual invests nature with more significance for the Hawaiian than that of an economic resource or a means of mere survival. The physical world communicates with them, and they see themselves as reflecting that world.[30]

Kanaloa, a god well-known in Hawaiian belief who has ties to the earth from its beginning, becomes the subject of a Merwin poem. With his spirits, Kanaloa rebelled against the great god Kāne, was sent to the underworld, and acted as leader of the first group of spirits to come to earth after its division from heaven. Kāne and Kanaloa are typically placed in legends as, respectively, the good and evil wishers of humankind. The parallels here to Kanaloa and the Christian devil are obvious, but Kanaloa and Kāne are also known as awa (a narcotic potion) drinkers, cultivators, and finders of springs of water for chiefs, giving them earthly attributes.[31] Further combining the natural and the spiritual, Kanaloa is the god of the squid, or octopus, and is associated with the sea.[32]

Merwin's poem, "Kanaloa," begins with the god's awakening to a universe propelled toward him as if a battle were approaching. The awakening of the god appears to be his realization of both the heaven-earth split and his arrival on earth: "When he woke his mind was the west / and he could not remember waking"; in every direction in which he looks, the sun, moon, and wind appear to be approaching him.[33] Kanaloa is not originally believed by the people in the poem, but as god of the underworld, his force is undeniable because he "houses the ghosts" of the trees, animals, whales, and insects.[34] The ineluctable quality of the god continues with "he rises in dust he is burning he is smoke" and "he is the coming home."[35] By the narrator ending with a claim that Kanaloa might "never have wakened," we are left with a puzzle rather than a sense of closure.[36] Our following responses to the last line might be, "What would have happened if the god had never awakened?" or, "What value is Merwin ascribing to deities?" The ambiguous ending, like the beginning, seems to reflect the often accidental character of the appearance and actions of deities in legend. Often unpredictable, gods are like the nature we should hold reverence for. Although nature may be forceful, even destructive, Native Hawaiians have understood that it is to be accepted, not conquered. A god of the underworld may seem a frightening prospect to the Euro-American reader, but in Hawaii this deity is seen and respected as a part of a cosmological framework. Like other Hawaiian deities, Kanaloa blends the physical with the spiritual in a way in which they cannot be separated without losing meaning for either one. In this ontology, the world is not simply a collection of phenomena, but, rather, a sacred ground for the enactment of the mysteries of life and death.

As mentioned earlier, the Kumulipo is an evolutionary Hawaiian chant permanently linking humans with the natural world. This creation story, according to Dudley, is strikingly different from that of the West, thereby shaping a worldview distinctly non-European:

> The Kumulipo traces evolutionary development through higher and higher species until it finally reaches man. After the Kumulipo reaches man, it traces the genealogy of the chiefs from the first man down to Lono-i-ka-makahiki, a chief reigning on the island of Hawai'i in the 17th century.

The chants of the Hawaiians told them that they had descended from the cosmos itself and from its many plant and animal species. They were related as family to all of the forms of nature from which they had descended. They felt a kinship with nature which is not experienced by people who see a break between mankind and the species of nature which have preceded them in the evolutionary advance. In the Western world, where the cleavage is most pronounced, animals are disdained as having senses but no reason; the plant world is recognized as alive, but in no way even aware; and the elements of the cosmos are treated as inert objects which follow mechanical laws. Hawaiians, on the other hand, view all of these beings as sentient ancestral forms which interrelate with them as family.[37]

A view of the earth, of the cosmos, that defines it as the foundation of humankind's existence allows for the reverence of not only living things but also of place. "Term," from *The Rain in the Trees*, describes what Merwin has seen of the loss of reverence for place in colonized Hawaii, as well as what may happen anywhere. The poem's title evokes the vocabulary of commerce; business operates on "terms." "Term" may also denote a limited extent of time—here, the end to a part of the natives' culture. Despite the shards of tradition remaining in respect to an ancient road in the poem, it will be eliminated with the rise of the new society.

"Term" informs us of the storytelling tradition of Native Hawaiian society—here, an old man tells his personal story of walking as a child on a road once built by a chief and how his father and grandfather walked with him along that same road, which seemed ageless. In contrast, in modern Hawaii skyrocketing real estate prices from over-development have forced large numbers of Native Hawaiians off of original grounds. In "Term," the native children will someday have to beg to visit the ocean because they are not "rich or foreign"; and when the last remnants of the traditions of place fade, the flourishing scene will become as spiritually empty as its despoilers: "where the thorny / kiawe trees smelling / of honey / dance in their shadows along the sand / the road will die / and turn into money at last."[38] The sharp irony of these lines runs throughout the poem in an indictment of notions of progress. Satirically, Merwin issues questions that are the corollary to a thinking that places no value on the natural world or on original culture by asking what is sacred about a road, a place, a language, or anything. "Term"'s message is one of finality. The result of the actions of the developers is a closing, an ending to what was indigenous, as the native people are excluded from areas that they cannot afford to enter. The narrator, linking past and present in full circle, associates this contemporary loss with the death legacy of the first European explorers whose ships brought little good to the Hawaiian people.

Merwin's idea for "Term" appears to have come from a controversy in Hawaii beginning in 1986 over the proposed building of a hotel over an ancient Hawaiian grave site in Maui. Construction of the hotel was not permitted by law until an excavation of the site at Honokahua was accomplished to determine its historic and cultural significance, but the excavation itself caused considerable turmoil because it involved disturbing the burial grounds. Excavations began in the summer of 1987, and by December 1988 the remains of nearly 1,000 burials of individuals and groups had been removed, as well as numerous artifacts of different ages. In addition, volcanic glass found at this location indicated that some of the bones were at least 1,000 years old and that some may have dated from A.D. 700. The Honokahua site also included a section of an old stone-paved road that might be part of the ancient King's Road, which once followed the perimeter of the island. Finally, in mid-1989 an agreement was reached among the Hawaiian activist group protesting the excavations, the Office of Hawaiian Affairs, the Hawaiian State Preservation Office, and the construction company of the hotel to rebury the ancient bones.[39]

In the poem, Merwin chooses not to address the entire issue, including the removal of the bones from the Honokahua site, but, rather, the impending loss of the sacred road. The road seemed to have always been there by the sea, having been built long ago by the chief, and will in the future be closed to all who are not rich or foreign. Given the history of the road and its proximity to the burial grounds, it is little wonder that Merwin would ask sardonically within the poem what is sacred about this road. Merwin's undisguised homily indicates that the development of an area of such cultural value to many Native Hawaiians into resort property signifies the perpetuation of imperialistic soullessness.

The cultural changes that have made possible loss in the Hawaiian environment have taken place in the last two centuries, a moment on the ecological time scale. The rapid damage to Hawaiian indigenous life has partially been inflicted by the implementation of Western methods of agriculture—particularly, the practice of large-scale farming. While walking down a hillside, the speaker of "Native" reflects upon the mules that transformed the island landscape into plowed fields when he was still a boy, and how, in three years' time, the soil had eroded and run into the ocean beyond "sea cliffs" and "frigate birds."[40] This harsh method of cultivating the land has replaced the original and the sacred, the 'ohia trees "filled with red flowers red birds / water notes flying music / the shining of the gods."[41] Now, surviving palm fronds exist side by side with chicken wire, and native plants sit in plastic pots where there was once a lush, mysterious wilderness. The indigenous or endemic species that the speaker re-plants are even labeled, ironically, with Latin names. Taking up the issue of Hawaiian plantations earlier than this, the three-page "Questions to Tourists Stopped by a Pineapple Field" from the 1983 volume, *Opening the Hand*, strings together question after question in the manner of a consumer marketing survey. Queries like "do you know whether the natives   ate pineapple?" and "what and where was the last   bird you noticed?" wryly indict the Euro-American populace that has come into Hawaii for industrial or recreational purposes.[42] The caesura, or broken-back line so often used in this volume, inserts a coy pause within the questions asked, and the straightforward mourning and polemics usually evident in the native poems is tempered here by a satiric imitation of the circulars of advertising executives. Yet, although the tone of this poem is more subtle, the underlying message remains constant. Death of native culture, lack of understanding of native environments, and change of native ecology all presage historic and natural loss.

In a 1984 interview, Merwin remarked that his contact with re-maining Hawaiian culture has been a great source of fulfillment to him, but that this relationship has heightened his conflict over the depletion of the natural world and the destruction of other cultures.[43] As evidence of the change that has happened in Hawaii, Merwin commented that when Captain Cook arrived, the flora and fauna there were almost entirely unique—almost all the species found in Hawaii had evolved there. Large-scale agriculture, however, has radi-cally damaged the natural environment of the islands.[44]

As a postscript to his poems of European conquerors, Merwin's *Travels* (1993) depicts several naturalists who journeyed to the New World on botanical quests. The poems continue to expose what colo-nization has done to indigenous species, but, perhaps more acutely, they demonstrate how the misguided enterprises damaged the natu-ralists who undertook them. Among them, "The Real World of Manuel

Córdova" gives an account of a rubber harvester in the Amazon who finally flees a native culture he cannot comprehend, a hostile environment he cannot reckon with, and a treacherous frontier capitalism. In "After Douglas," David Douglas, namesake of the Douglas fir, is trampled by a bull in a pit on Mauna Kea, Hawaii. In "Cinchona," Richard Spruce battles sickness and a violent river in Ecuador while attempting to transplant cinchona plants (the source of quinine) to India, where they perished.[45]

The attitudes that people have about the land that they live on are, to this poet, the best indicators of its future. Merwin has pointed out that somewhere in his journals Thoreau spoke of his grief at the enclosure of the Concord Common, an event that would prevent people from allowing their animals to roam there and would eliminate huckleberry picking. Then, the land would belong to somebody and would no longer be free.[46] With treatment of the land as resource, as in the enclosure of the Concord Common, the process of loss begins even though it may be discernible only to a few. Respect for the natural world, for the history and attitudes of indigenous cultures regarding their environment, and for the indigenous cultures themselves go hand in hand. What may be termed progress by expansionists may also be the foundation for a loss that is irreversible.

The Vanishing Planet

Merwin began his poetry of ecological loss with *The Lice* in 1967 by writing of the disappearing animals of the earth. His poems that specifically target environmental damage, along with his poems of the settling of New World lands and the conquering of native cultures, represent a significant segment of Merwin's canon and one of his most important subjects from his personal viewpoint. Because Merwin is so personally involved in this issue, many of these poems are bitter or ironic in tone. To Merwin, ecological damage must be dealt with in a polemic manner because it is so serious a subject and so irreversible an action.

The Lice, Merwin's most popular volume with critics, contains several poems that address the depletion of animal populations. Perhaps Merwin's most famous conservationist piece from *The Lice* is "For a Coming Extinction," which addresses the gray whale before its imminent disappearance. The sharp irony of the poem comes across quickly as the recklessness and self-importance of our attitudes are spelled out for us:

> Gray whale
> Now that we are sending you to The End
> That great god
> Tell him
> That we who follow you invented forgiveness
> And forgive nothing
>
> . . . .
> When you have left the seas nodding on their stalks
> Empty of you
> Tell him that we were made
> On another day[1]

Merwin takes on the role of ecoprophet in the poem, confronting us with what we are doing to the animals of the planet and our subsequent denial of responsibility. Our Judeo-Christian religious heritage tells us that we are moral creatures able to conceive "forgive-ness" and that we were created differently from the animals. Yet, with his own theologically laden homily, Merwin refutes the notion of a sacred right of dominion over other forms of life and images the animals' deaths as grotesque "sacrifices." The poem closes with more echoes of our very thoughts, if not our words, of our prominence in the scheme of things:

> When you will not see again
> The whale calves trying the light
> Consider what you will find in the black garden
> And its court
> The sea cows the Great Auks the gorillas
> The irreplaceable hosts ranged countless
> And fore-ordaining as stars
> Our sacrifices
>
> . . . . . .
> Tell him
> That it is we who are important[2]

One of the effects of such poetry is to cause us to consider animals as other beings, capable of a thought and communication of their own. When asked by Ed Folsom whether he gives voice to the "voice-less beings" so that they may express their rage against human culture, Merwin responded with both a yes and a no:

> It would be very presumptuous to agree to that, but insofar as I dare to suggest a formula for myself or anyone else, I think it's very important to remain open to that possibility, to welcome it, and to evoke it if possible. Otherwise, what else is there? Otherwise, one is there in an ego-bound, historical, culturally brainwashed, incredibly limited moment. One can't perceive anything because one has no perspective at all. The opposite—the nearest thing I can imagine to what I would think of as a sound or even healthy approach and attitude toward existence as a whole (as distinct from the endless separation of the human species from the rest of existence that leads to evaluating the one at the expense of the other)—would be Blake's "How do you know but ev'ry Bird that cuts the airy way, / Is an immense world of delight, clos'd to your senses five?" It works both ways, one both can be and can never be the bird.[3]

This espousal of an openness to possibility without the certainty of knowledge is the same as what we found when analyzing the concept of origin. Without Blake's imaginative leap we are isolated within our species; yet, at the same time, we must recognize the limits of knowing other species. By making animals part of our consciousness, by making them part of our myth, a project is engaged that may be invaluable, not for its expression of our beliefs through animals, but for our reevaluation of our relationship to one another.

This relationship serves as the basis of "In Autumn," also from *The Lice.* Dramatized is the destruction of a livable habitat for humans when the world has lost its animal populations. Although what is missing is presented from the narrator's, and thereby the human's, point of view, the loss is for all creatures. "In Autumn" begins after the death of the animals, who are seeking a home that has been taken from them and will never be returned:

> The extinct animals are still looking for home
> . . . .
>
> Now they will
> Never arrive
>
> The stars are like that
>
> Moving on without memory
> Without having been near turning elsewhere climbing
> Nothing the wall
> . . . .
> The lights are going on in the leaves nothing to do with evening
>
> Those are cities
> Where I had hoped to live[4]

Still on a journey after they have been exterminated, the animals are like stars whose past light is all that we see of them. They will never find a resting place, and the entire milieu, apparently the entire universe, exemplifies emptiness and displacement. In the closing lines, the speaker says that he had "hoped to live" within certain "cities"—which I take to figuratively signify communities in the natural world. The animals' extermination is like losing a place where he might have existed with some sense of wholeness. The terse phrases and disjointed completions of thoughts amplify the poem's anxiety and reveal for us the poet's despair during its writing. Much of the content, like that of other poems from *The Lice,* builds a grim, nearly hopeless perspective. Even the opening poem from the volume, "The Animals," initiates the mood of alienation repeated throughout it: "And myself tracking over empty ground / Animals I never saw."[5]

Maxine Kumin, a contemporary of Merwin, considers the tragedy of extinct or endangered species in her 1989 volume of poetry, *Nurture.* Here, the caribou, manatee, Aleutian goose, arctic fox, killer whale, trumpeter swan, dusky seaside sparrow, and others are presented as examples of nature's victims to humankind. Kumin presents an interesting case when she laments the conversion of wildlife into pets to satisfy our ego demands for domination. "Repent" describes this behavior, as exercised upon the killer whale: "And when we've captured two or three / we pen them in a little jail / and teach them tricks / to do for fishy snacks / for paying multitudes who fill // the stands and scream to see / these mammals leap in synchrony."[6] She forcefully makes her point when she turns the moral ledger toward us: "Stu-/ pidity, said / Immanuel Kant, / is caused by a wicked / heart. Repent."[7] One Kumin poem on species extinction considers the last dusky seaside sparrow on the day of its reported death, along with other vanishing animals: "Tomorrow we can put it on a stamp, / a first-day cover with Key Largo rat, / Schaus swallowtail, Florida swamp / crocodile, and fading cotton mouse. / How simply symbols replace habitat!"[8] Like Merwin's "For a Coming Extinction," Kumin chooses to catalog other extinct or nearly extinct species to make her case for the existence of a pattern of destruction of biodiversity.

What we replace the biotic community with are reflections of the human mind. Our creations, proud of them though we may be, are merely "symbols" of the once-living landscape, poor replacements for a former home: "The tower frames at Aerospace / quiver in the flush of another shot / where, once indigenous, the dusky sparrow / soared trilling twenty feet above its burrow."[9] Kumin's volume continues Merwin's charge in *The Lice* that out of arrogance we have robbed the animals of their homes (and thereby their lives) and we have robbed the planet of much of its natural wealth.

Two years before the publication of *The Lice,* Merwin wrote a review for *The Nation* of four books concerning the use or protection of animals. The review, which he entitled "On the Bestial Floor," reminds us of the past's belief in the biblical exhortation for humans to have dominion over the earth and its creatures. It also notes that this spiritual and intellectual superiority, passed down to modern man, has failed to manifest itself in the ability for him to rule himself:

Now in the rare instances where his convenience alone is not taken as ample justification for his manipulations and erasures of other species, it is his intelligence, or some aspect of it, that is held up most regularly as the great exoneration. This, according to the myth, was the property which gave him the edge on other creatures; and in the process it became endowed, in his eyes, with a spontaneous moral splendor which now constitutes between him and the rest of nature not a relative but an absolute difference, like the one which separates him from the silence. Indeed, by now, this difference and its exigencies are normally deferred to like the great necessities themselves, as though they were not only ordained but everlasting.... And yet as man's power over other living things has become, if not more perfect at least more pervasive, his dominion over himself, however conceived, seems here and there to be escaping him despite analyses and institutions, and taking, it may be, the route of the departed divinity.[10]

Merwin's religious position is a departure from that of his avowed philosophical mentor, Thoreau, whose writings express a belief in the God of Christianity despite his scorn for his townspeople's orthodox religion. Another obvious difference lies in Merwin's continuing interest in Buddhism, which rejects the notion of an externalized deity. Yet, Merwin and Thoreau's agreement in their love of nature and in their concern for it bind them to another sort of "faithful" impulse—the urge to preserve what is disappearing.

Donald Worster asserts that Thoreau, faced with the events of American history and the rapidly changing New England landscape around him, felt his sense of trust in the Old World models of a permanent and hardy nature eroding. Thoreau's primary purpose in his ecological studies was to discover the true state of the country before the Europeans' settling.[11] This, then, may largely explain the passage in *Walden* of reverence for native peoples that we have examined in the chapter on origin. Because these early peoples were tied to a more pristine earth, they may have signified to the nineteenth-century writer a class of caretakers of the land, a group whose guardianship stood in opposition to the rapidly advancing machine of American industry and whose presence may have been more moral, more religious, than that of Europeans.

In Merwin's work it is plain that with our increased technological power an increased desire for the animal kingdom to behave according to our expectations of it has arisen. "Fly" depicts the owner of a pigeon who wishes his pet to fly, all the while ignoring the fact that it has been kept in a dovecote, which has caused the bird to lose its ability

and desire to do so. The narrator cannot at first associate this result
with his own actions:

> I have been cruel to a fat pigeon
> Because he would not fly
> All he wanted was to live like a friendly old man
>
> He had let himself become a wreck filthy and confiding
> Wild for his food beating the cat off the garbage
>
> . . . .
>
> *Fly* I said throwing him into the air
> But he would drop and run back expecting to be fed
> I said it again and again throwing him up[12]

What finally causes the narrator to realize the mistake in his thinking
is the death of the bird, a tragic circumstance when this poem is read
as a parable of all living things. The narrator's recognition of his
egocentrism and anthropocentrism comes as a great shock to him—as
if he first becomes aware of his true self. With the realization of the
import of his actions comes his awareness of how he, as all humans,
has used language to perpetuate his aggression: "So that is what I
am // Pondering his eye that could not / Conceive that I was a
creature to run from // I who have always believed too much in
words."[13] Merwin may intend the last line of the poem to serve as a
particular warning to himself, because he is a poet, and because writers
place special value upon language. However, we all place value upon
language—too much value when the words are used as excuses for
exploitation or as a dividing line between ourselves and other species
in an "absolute" fashion.

A parallel poem to "Fly" appears on the page immediately preceding
it in *The Lice*. "Death of a Favorite Bird" also treats a bird made into
a pet, but this time, instead of the narrator trying to force the bird
to regain its natural abilities, the bird risks everything to achieve its
original state. Despite his obtuse pondering, the truth of what the
narrator of "Death of A Favorite Bird" has done eventually comes to
haunt him in the memory of the bird's suffering:

> What was the matter with life on my shoulder
>
> . . . .
>
> That you had to thresh out your breath in the spiked rafters
> To the beat of rain
> I have asked this question before it knows me it comes

Back to find me through the cold dreamless summer
And the barn full of black feathers[14]

In a situation remarkably similar in a Keats poem, "I had a dove, and the sweet dove died," Keats's narrator cannot understand why his pet could not exist happily, separate from the forest, and has died of grief. Keats's narrator, however, appears to be missing any sort of recognition of his culpability. Like the life "on [the] shoulder," Keats's speaker has kept the dove's feet tied with a silken cord, and the poem may very well be the inspiration for both "Fly" and "Death of a Favorite Bird."

Adding to the species-centeredness of the narrators, noteworthy in the two poems is the irreversible doom for the birds. Treating animals as objects is not something that has its chances of working out in Merwin's view—it will assuredly extinguish them eventually. Merwin had good reason for such suppositions at the time these poems were written. In the 1960s, widespread information was beginning to appear before the general public about the extinction of several species from the planet at once and about pervasive industrial and chemical pollution, most notably with Rachel Carson's 1962 *Silent Spring*, a study of pesticide abuses in America. At the present, an even greater media attention is being paid to threatened animal and plant populations, pollution, and damage to the earth and atmosphere, yet massive numbers of people in the United States still wish to deny the existence of any type of ecological problem. The intensity of many of the arguments points to an unwillingness to believe that past modes of conceiving the world may be destructive and that humans may be capable of such horrendous ecocide or, perhaps, suicide. The notion that America is still a land to be explored and harvested for its resources with little heed for the future thrives in the presence of a moral certitude.

The Lice, then, actually predicts many of the real-world events to follow three decades later and, more than any other book of Merwin, stands as his commentary on environmental damage. It is noteworthy that the volume, with its postapocalyptic viewpoint, should actually precede by many years any universal confirmation among nonscientists that such a problem could or might exist. However, the volume was not Merwin's only publication at the time on the subject. In the decade in which *The Lice* was published, the poet wrote numerous prose pieces having to do with our earthly plight.

"Letter from Aldermaston" (1960) describes the 1960 Aldermaston to London Nuclear Disarmament March, in which Merwin took part.

"Act of Conscience" (1962) details the sailing of the *Everyman* in 1962 in protest of nuclear tests around Christmas Island and the following demonstrations and trial. "The Terrible Meek," from the same year, records the arrest and trial of elderly Quaker antinuclear demonstrators. "A New Right Arm" (1963) delivers a satiric suggestion in the tradition of Swift's "A Modest Proposal" for the use of atomic mutants in the military. Also, as we have already seen, "On the Bestial Floor" (1965) outlines the history of humankind's ontological division of itself from animals. Especially during the time that *The Lice* was written, and immediately before that, Merwin was feeling strongly about what humankind was doing and was questioning whether there was any hope for changing the status quo. While living in England during the late fifties and in early 1960, he was associated with the Committee of Nuclear Disarmament and the Committee of a Hundred, another antinuclear group. His activity there, which included participating in the Aldermaston to London marches, gave him a qualified sense of hope about the future. The Cuban Missile Crisis, however, which occurred while he was living in New York in the early sixties, ended his expectations. In the Clifton interview, he outlines how these political developments affected his writing:[15]

> But really, the thing that followed, that came out of it, was the very end of *The Moving Target* and then a good bit of *The Lice*. I suppose that's a part of the darkness of *The Lice*. The feeling that as a nation and a species we were involved—and one is never involved completely unconsciously, some of this is deliberate and conscious—possibly helplessly involved in a kind of lemming race. We're just trying to destroy ourselves. And one of the forms it took was trying to destroy the other forms of life around us.[16]

The atmospheric tests in the Pacific, the missile crisis, and open suggestions of aggression toward Russia and Cuba that Merwin heard people professing while he was living in New York were a significant source of distress to the poet. However, these political tensions and the treatment of the environment, ironically, prompted him to seek out remaining possibilities:

> I thought, "I wake up every morning knowing what I hate. If someone asks me how would you live if you could live the way you wanted to, I wouldn't have a very good answer." And I thought, "Well, I better find out. That is just as important as knowing what the dangers are." So I lived differently for a number of years, and I suppose that is part of the answer.

You can be angry about what's happening to animals or to the whole of northern Canada or to the Amazon basin, or you can turn it around and think, "Well in the limited time left, why not pay attention to other people and to animals and to what's there?"[17]

His change in living involved moving to a farm in rural France in 1963. (He had already spent some time moving back and forth between France and New York.) However, not until the publication of *The Carrier of Ladders* (1970) would Merwin's readers begin to find a change in tone, as in its pages he periodically offered moments of promise through his literary naturism. After the bitterness of the early sixties left him, he did not turn a blind eye toward the environmental problem or cease to have times when he became vocal about it. His continued concern for environmental integrity forms a major component of *The Rain in the Trees* and is the basis for numerous poems and prose pieces since *The Lice*.

The more discursive and less acidic poetry of *Opening the Hand* contains the poem "Shaving Without a Mirror," which both celebrates nature and laments its destruction. Near their middle point, the lines of the poem contain a caesura, or internal break, which is common to Old English verse and which Merwin uses in several poems in the volume. The narrator celebrates the living world by contemplating a mountain scene and the surrounding skies. Along with his observation, he attempts remembrance of his connection to the place; he longs for original psychic ties to it. The tone quickly changes, however, when he begins musing upon loss to the natural world and his subsequent personal loss: "where are the forest voices   now that the forests have gone / and those from above the treeline ... when did I ever knowingly   set hands on a cloud."[18] The narrator includes himself in communal wrongdoing, realizing that he is part of the race that has been responsible for the damage, and he expresses his fear for the future because children now have no sense of a wild nature: "*Brother the world is blind   and surely you come from it* / where children grow steadily   without knowledge of creatures // other than domesticated."[19]

This mingling of joy over nature and a mourning of its dismantling also appears in "Before Us," where the speaker and his lover are experiencing the final moments remaining on the natural calendar. Much has already been lost—"the Laughing Owls ... and honeycreepers and the brown / bears of Atlas / the white wolf and the sea mink have not been seen / by anyone living."[20] Despite the loss of species, damage to the land, and the disappearance of native ideologies, the two lovers will, nevertheless, find something of the original world left, symbolically and literally, with the return of morning. The narrator in "Shaving Without a Mirror" cannot overcome loss in this manner, and he is so overwhelmed by it that he questions his very being: "I stand by a line of trees   staring at a bare summit / do I think I was born here   I was never born."[21] Disenfranchisement prompts him to try to remember the pastoral, a farm before the "war," but his desire cannot dispel his grief.[22] The brighter ending of "Before Us" apparently has to do with the narrator's facing the natural end with his lover, however short the time left may be. In "Shaving Without a Mirror" the solitary self is vexed to near collapse by the destruction of the earth.[23]

Interestingly, "Before Us" recalls some of Merwin's more political works from *The Moving Target* and *The Lice* with its charges of political injustice: "where were you when the lies were voting / and the fingers believed faces on money"[24] is reminiscent of "And your lies elected // They return in the same / Skins to the same seats by the flags of money" from "For Now."[25] In "Before Us" the political past is offered because it marks the years that the narrator and his lover have lived through but spent apart—they have come together rather late in life—but the passage has further meaning. Government's lack of concern, if not outright opposition to environmental efforts, has contributed to the current dilemma. With the poetry focusing on the conquering of New World lands, that which clearly opposes our actions in Vietnam, and the poetry of environmental loss, it is evident that politics is a part of the scope of this "deep image" poet. Furthermore, more direct political commentary is often found in the essays. So, the origin poetry, cloaked in mystery and ostensibly apolitical, and the environmental loss poems, unmistakable in their instructional intention, typify different though common naturist approaches in Merwin. Although these rhetorical techniques are different, the ideology engendering them is identical: as mystery or as endangered entity, nature is depicted as a part of our very being, to be protected for that fact as well as for its own sake.

The prose poems of Merwin are no doubt his most difficult works to interpret. For their degree of surrealism many are quite obscure, and these pieces have been abandoned more often than not by critics. Yet, the poet has one prose poem, "Unchopping a Tree," which clearly, through satire, takes up the cause of ecological loss. Here, Merwin reveals his position in a subtle, nondidactic manner, and the irony of the entire piece may help us understand what he works for in his lyrical poems. On the surface, "Unchopping a Tree" seriously offers a set of instructions for those who wish to put trees back together after they have already been cut down. The procedures that Merwin delineates for accomplishing this task are as specific as any one might find in an assembly manual:

> Start with the leaves, the small twigs, and the nests that have been shaken, ripped, or broken off by the fall; these must be gathered and attached once again to their respective places. It is not arduous work, unless major limbs have been smashed or mutilated. . . . It goes without saying that if the tree was hollow in whole or in part, and contained old nests of bird or mammal or insect, or hoards of nuts or such structures as wasps or bees build for their survival, the contents will have to be repaired where necessary, and reassembled, insofar as possible, in their original order, including the shells of nuts already opened.[26]

Included in the directions for this rebuilding are how to put spiders' webs and leaves back on the tree as well as is possible; how to raise the trunk by means of a scaffolding; how to put the splinters, chips, and sawdust back together; and how to remove the delicate scaffolding. Merwin's intricate list of the steps necessary to put a tree back together whimsically makes us realize the complexity of an organism like a tree and the impossiblity of undoing certain damage. Ironically, the animals have the ability to repair such injury better than humans, but in this case they decline, because they have gathered from experience to stay out of humans' way:

> Even in the best of circumstances it is a labor that will make you wish often that you had won the favor of the universe of ants, the empire of mice, or at least a local tribe of squirrels, and could enlist their labors and their talents. But no, they leave you to it. They have learned, with time. This is men's work.[27]

In the final few lines of the poem, Merwin asks twice, "What more can you do?"[28] The following answer, unfortunately, is that "there is nothing more you can do."[29] After enough ecological destruction, the efforts to restore the earth are ultimately as futile as trying to put a tree back together after it has been cut down. Merwin's closing lines—"Others are waiting. Everything is going to have to be put back"—predict that our widespread damage to the environment will require universal efforts for healing.[30]

"Trees," from *The Compass Flower*, similarly takes up the subject of trees as emblematic of ecological loss, mixing anger and sorrow with a sense of remaining joy in much the same fashion as "Shaving Without a Mirror" and "Before Us." In this poem, the trees have previously stood unharmed on any scale by humankind's appropriative act of naming them, but they are now destined to fall. The memory of a safer time in childhood, a time of the imagination, is the only solace available: "they have stood round my sleep / and when it was forbidden to climb them / they have carried me in their branches."[31] Yet, memory and desire, although useful in the poems of origin, cannot bridge the gap between the wished-for and the actual in the poems portraying ecological decline. Love for the natural world has led Merwin to spend much of his life in rural areas, yet by living in these areas he has seen firsthand what recklessness has done to them. Although Merwin would like to live in an environment where nature has not been tainted—the purity of origin—this is not the condition of much of the countryside today. The city and the country are not opposites in the ecological situation, but different sides of the same coin, as he explained in a 1991 interview:

> ... the country is not to me just a sort of alternate to the city. Oddly enough, they both remind me of the arrogance of our kind in different ways. In the city I'm aware of how much we take for granted, how much we're dependent upon and we just take it for granted that that's O.K. In the country one sees it happening, you know, you see the forests being destroyed and the place being strip mined and so forth. And of course the natural world will survive us, but it will survive us in a very badly scarred and for a while depleted way, and it's too bad that we do that to it.[32]

The poems of origin make it plain that nature is an essential part of our psychological and spiritual well-being. Yet, there are few poems in which Merwin discusses the role of nature in our lives on a more physical level, when he writes of a world literally falling away beneath our feet, or when he describes the tangible harm that our inventions are doing to us. "The Crust," from *The Rain in the Trees*, depicts a world that is physically coming apart due to changes made upon it. "The Crust" harks back somewhat to Merwin's first few books of poems, many of which had medieval settings. In this poem, a servant or apprentice addresses his master with a diction evoking the Middle Ages—as "Sire"; however, the situation is clearly modern. The narrator relates that on a holiday during the summer, when traffic was congested, he witnessed a road collapsing due to the earth falling away from underneath it.[33]

The narrator explains to his superior that he tried to get the people to go back as the road split open and that some complied. Yet, this proves to be a measure taken too late. After the cutting of a tree, the earth caves away as all life dependent upon the tree is also extinguished: "and with the tree / went all the lives in it / .... for whom it was all there was."[34] Merwin's concept of nature having a "language" all its own, as in "After the Alphabets" and "Tracing the Letters," appears here with the tree having "evolved the only language," and in the tree's having "remembered everything" recollection again plays a part.[35] These characteristic attributes are lost with the tree, though, and the mock humility of the servant builds the bitter satire in his message concerning the universal results of individual acts as he concludes, "but what do I know I am only a witness" and as he points out that the earth is also eroding from underneath his master's chair.[36] The wisdom of the servant, much like the disguised truths spoken by fools in Shakespeare's plays, derides the notion that those who are in authority, even our own authorities, act justly by virtue of their office. As in some of the poems with Native American or Native Hawaiian subjects, it is often the powerless who are in a position to recognize the consequences of the actions of the powerful.

By taking up the question of whether humans can live without nature, Merwin deliberately deals from a stacked deck. Of course, the answer is "no," but the poet earnestly wishes his readers to ponder his simple point. According to ecocentric thinking, when we eradicate nature we also literally eradicate ourselves, for we are only one part of an ecosystem in which all things must thrive for us to thrive also. Scientific experiments to create artificial products from clothing to foods have only been partially successful; there is no workable "natureless" paradigm, and science is more and more acknowledging the absolute interconnectedness of life on the planet. Although we may cling to the concept that our inventions are always for the good, sometimes, as Merwin points out in "The Superstition," the opposite is true. "The Superstition" takes as its title a word that we associate with the ancient, the anachronistic, and the ill-informed. Here, belief is in the automobile, a relatively new device in our race to outdesign nature. When inventions' shortcomings in comparison to their myths come to light, we are left with the sobering knowledge that we have deceived ourselves. Initially believing that automobiles would "save" our lives, we have arrived at the awareness of how many lives we have lost to them: "we dreamed of them and we woke / with the headlights flying through us."[37]

"The Crust" and "The Superstition" appear in *The Rain in the Trees;* yet going back as far as *The Lice,* poetry of the physical effects of environmental change upon humans may be found. *The Lice's* explicit condemnation of human action upon nature implicitly voices a warning about the nature-deprived world into which we are forcing ourselves. In "The Finding of Reasons" it is "the string of the great kite Sapiens" that "Cuts our palms / Along predestined places."[38] The "future" of the gray whale in "For a Coming Extinction" will be "Dead," but so will "ours."[39]

Environmental danger to people, the near-extinction of certain animals, greed, political corruption, and national self-righteousness all coalesce in Merwin's apocalyptic *The Lice.* Since that 1967 volume, much more information has been released to the general public about ecological damage, and most of it is foreboding. Merwin gave more recent thoughts on the topic and what his feelings about the future are in a 1989 interview:

> I think that what we as a species have been doing for a long time is so destructive that it may have passed points of no return already. And that we . . . may not be able to survive in the world (our species), life probably will. To me it's a really doubtful point whether we will or won't. . . . you know we're not very far from terrible air pollution and water pollution and all of these things—and there are lots of ways, through overpopulation and the spread of diseases and things that we can't control, that we may destroy ourselves. And I think that we are destroying the environment at a rate that we may not be able to survive. . . . I don't have a very strong sense of the future, you know.[40]

Perhaps the most bizarre situation that can be portrayed in literature is when a person or group of people pursue that which will certainly bring about their doom, for no redeeming purpose. A dramatic example appears in Melville's *Moby-Dick* when the mariners, bewitched by Ahab's maniacal passion, follow him to their deaths. The thoughts and actions of humans in "Thanks" may not be so spectacular as chasing after a deadly whale, but the result is as disastrous. Caught up in the myth of the machine, we continue to pay homage to our inventions as they destroy us. "Thanks" demonstrates the pervasiveness of the program that has held industry and profit up as our ideals and the difficulty of rejecting such idols even in the face of their tragic consequences. People in "Thanks" express their gratitude outside or on elevators, after they have been to funerals or during telephone conversations, in the midst of violence or in the comfort of wealth. In short, we believe that our present-day world offers us a better existence than ever before because we expect it to, and we therefore do not question it.

"Thanks," like "Before Us," calls to mind many of the poems from *The Lice*, with its mention of political corruption and greed as it consciously invokes the climate of the sixties—"remembering wars and the police at the door."[41] Similar to the poetry that treats the history of our environmental destruction, "Thanks" draws upon this past to explain why the crisis is happening. The chain of corruption and misuse of technology has remained unbroken over the years, and the evidence of this upon the natural world is everywhere. A society that has been blinded, that is void of the ability to scrutinize its ills, may have no perception of its place in a larger biosphere:

> with the animals dying around us
> taking our feelings we are saying thank you
> with the forests falling faster than the minutes
> of our lives we are saying thank you
> with the words going out like cells of a brain[42]

When he writes of the animals and the trees in the poem, Merwin links them psychically to us. With the animals' deaths, they take "our feelings" with them; the death of the forests happens simultaneously with the loss of time from our own lives; and the entire process spurs a loss of self-contact and articulation that is likened to mental deterioration. Enough exposure to propaganda about the perfection of society makes automatons of us, unable to see the falling forests and our own depletion of self.

This inversion of expectation and actuality is a typical motif in Merwin. His penchant for irony and twists finds ample opportunity with the ecological issue, which, to the poet, is laden with misconceptions. In "To the Insects," Merwin inverts our position in nature's hierarchy, or what we perceive as our position. Envisioning what the future world will be like, Merwin addresses the lowliest of creatures as "Elders." As we have already seen, "After the Alphabets" depicts insects, not humans, as the future purveyors of language. Here, Merwin casts them to expose our own destructiveness by revealing how brief our existence on this planet has been and how species oriented we are. The irony of our psychological distinction of ourselves from the insects is that, like them, we are consuming the natural world. Killing the insects because they are sometimes pests, we nevertheless mirror them by "eating the forests / eating the earth and the water."[43] Our process will, however, eventually remove us from the planet, leaving only the lowly insects, who will own the "morning" with its "antiquity."[44]

To create a list of the poems in which our expectations of technology and development are ultimately dashed is, in effect, to list almost all of the ecological loss poems. Merwin repeatedly depicts our epistemology in order to show the inescapable link between thinking and reality. The continuing delusion that the earth is an inexhaustible resource permits the political and industrial complex to effect massive depletion and pollution for short-term gain. In juxtaposition, the belief of nineteenth-century Americans in their destiny to settle and mold the continent from coast to coast seems little worse than our own greed. Rarely will readers find a poem of environmental loss by Merwin that excludes the attitudinal connection.

As we examine Merwin's work, especially *The Rain in the Trees*, we discover that the poet's relationship to his home has strongly influenced his writings about ecological conditions. Merwin has been particularly interested in the Hawaiian Islands' ecology as well as their historical colonization. Hawaii has truly become Merwin's bioregion, that area with its own particular life forms, topography, and culture.[45] Specific environmental issues concerning Hawaii that Merwin has commented on include the Navy's bombing of the uninhabited island of Kahoolawe, the Navy's dumping of nuclear waste in Honolulu Harbor, the incipient destruction of the Wao Kele O Puna Rain Forest to make way for geothermal exploration, and the radical loss of native plant and animal species due to development and large-scale agriculture.[46]

In a plea for the Wao Kele O Puna Rain Forest that appeared in *The American Poetry Review* in 1990, Merwin stressed the importance of maintaining a rarity in American biology, a tropical lowland rainforest, for its inherent value:

The name of the forest is Wao Kele O Puna.... when the bulldozers moved in on it, in the autumn of 1989, it was no longer very large—some 27,000 acres. But it is the largest intact bit of lowland rain forest remaining in the Hawaiian islands, and it is unique. A few imported species have established themselves in it, around the edges, but for the most part the flora—much of it still unexplored—is composed entirely of native species evolved in the Hawaiian islands, in the process that makes these islands, from the biologists' point of view, one of the most remarkable sources on the planet. The Wao Kele O Puna, besides, is the only place in the islands where native birds, wiped out everywhere else in the lowlands, have managed to survive and to develop immunity to the avian malaria that arrived with the Europeans and the mosquito.[47]

Merwin's letter continues to explain that the Wao Kele O Puna is part of the "ceded lands" that were legally allotted to the use of the Hawaiian people, but that it was exchanged for a segment of nonnative forest by the State of Hawaii to permit the development. The Wao Kele O Puna also serves as a native touchstone to the Hawaiians for its support of indigenous flora like the great ohia trees and various plants used by practitioners of Native Hawaiian medicine.[48] These characteristics tie natural significance to cultural significance, observed in many of Merwin's Hawaiian poems, such as "Losing a Language," "Hearing the Names of the Valleys," and "Native."

Emphasizing the universality of loss of this sort in the face of the conquerors' myopia, "Chord" describes the cutting of some of the Hawaiian forests at the moment that Keats was writing his great odes. As Keats and the rest of Western civilization were busy with their more local endeavors, colonial expansion impacted a landscape far away: "While Keats wrote they were cutting down the sandalwood forests / while he listened to the nightingale they heard their own axes echoing through the forests."[49]

Striking about this poem is its focus on the culture implementing the invasion, specifically, one unwitting member of it, as it also describes the hardships of those sent to colonize Hawaii in a way that underscores the overall waste of the event: "while he felt his heart they were hungry and their faith was sick."[50] Keats knows nothing of the cutting of the Hawaiian forest as he extols nature in his poetry, as the Hawaiians begin to lose their natural environment, and the men sent to do the actual taking appear as nothing more than oppressed servants. "Chord"'s closing line, "and an age arrived when everything was explained in another language," introduces the disappearance of genuine connections to nature by means of an imported culture.[51] From this moment forward, the land will be seen from the viewpoint of outsiders, and the original inhabitants' perspective will be lost.

The cutting of the Hawaiian forest removed the original state of the land and its people—"an age of leaves and feathers"—and was in turn followed by the period of colonial domination.[52] Ecological events in Hawaii then followed a lightning-speed destructive current, evidenced by the rapid succession of varieties of trees taken and the rapid alteration of land type:

> someone dead
> thought of this mountain as money
> and cut the trees
> that were here in the wind
> in the rain at night
> it is hard to say it
> but they cut the sacred 'ohias then
> the sacred koas then
> the sandalwood and the halas
> holding aloft their green fires
> and somebody dead turned cattle loose
> among the stumps until killing time[53]

The logging in the passage is all the more tragic because of the temporality of the exploiters' goals, exposed with the repeated characterization of them as "dead." The poet describes the crippled forest, now, making another attempt at resurrection, although time is running out for this region and for all regions: "but the trees have risen one more time / ... the rain is falling on the last place."[54]

Merwin, obviously, is not hopeful about the future. Yet, despite his fears for the environment, his poetry reveals a remaining thread of possibility that humans may reverse their actions. However, as he mentioned in the interview with Michael Clifton, we must begin to recognize our biological bonds to the planet:

I'm not really interested in going to the moon. The earth is still a very beautiful place; it's seldom enough that it's seen. It's seen as an object of exploitation, rather than as something of which we are a part. We are neither superior nor inferior, we are a part of it. It is not different from us. So when we treat it with contempt and we exploit it, we are despising and exploiting ourselves.[55]

I first proposed that the search for origin may bring a sense of personal harmony with the earth and may initiate ecocentric thinking even though attainment of idyllic terrains is impossible. The origin poems place the poet (and, thereby the reader) into the process of making connections with the real living world. Attainment of the "mythical world" is not expected by the poet; finding and interacting with what remains of it is. The goal of biocentric existence, however, is threatened with defeat before the quest for it gets underway if the body of the earth continues to be depleted and contaminated on a daily basis. As the previous quotation indicates, the body of the earth is in a very tangible sense our body. Thoreau's work of the mid-nineteenth century represents an early literary ecology emphasizing organicism. Now, with the present-day writing of Merwin and others, celebrations of holism regularly include apocalyptic censure.

Writing about such matters, though, no matter how foreboding the message may be, indicates that for the poet there is possibility. The antihumanism of *The Lice* is tempered to a large degree by a reverence of native values and the healing capabilities of the natural world by the time of the publication of *The Rain in the Trees.* John Elder remarks that in the farmer's fields, in that "natural" area scarred by human intervention, Wendell Berry sees the "earth's wound and its healing."[56] Traces of this sort of Berry-esque desire for the reconciliation between humanity and the living world survive in Merwin. Even Merwin's strongest condemnations of human action imply a desire for reversal, although "most of the stories have to do with vanishing."[57]

The poet's source of sustenance is the earth, and in the process of creating poetry about the earth Merwin attempts to offer to his readers part of its wonder, part of its need. Current ecothinking holds that we are at a point in history where we must finally respect the planet. Abusing the earth for our own gains and perpetuating the anthropocentrism of the past is no longer possible, even from the narrow perspective of our own success. As the earth's wild places fall out of existence in disturbing proportions, individual actions take on monumental significance. In his poetry of ecological loss, Merwin the activist writes for the possibiilty that humankind may reexamine its course and that the remaining natural world may survive, as it is, a little while longer.

Notes

Chapter 1. Origin

1. Edward Hirsch, introduction to "The Art of Poetry XXXVIII: W. S. Merwin," *Paris Review* 29, no. 102 (1987): 57–58; Gina Maranto, "A Tender of Trees: W. S. Merwin's Poetry and Politics, " *Amicus Journal* 14, no. 1 (1992): 13–14.

2. Lawrence Buell, *The Environmental Imagination: Thoreau, Nature Writing, and the Formation of American Culture* (Cambridge, Mass.: Belknap Press, 1995), 35.

3. Ibid., 44. Buell identifies the pastoral with the artistic representation and remythification of the natural environment. In his discussion on the pastoral, he explains how it may validly deliver nature to and promote nature consciousness in the reader, or how it may abstract readers from it. Even within the same work, these contrary ideological strains are often present (31, 50–52).

4. Ibid., 50. I will sometimes use Buell's term "literary naturism" or "naturism" as an additional term to refer to nature writing. As Buell points out, "naturalism" is inappropriate for the genre because it implies "a more restrictively (proto)scientific approach" and has the further problem of being associated with a school of social representation in the works of such writers as Émile Zola, Theodore Dreiser, and August Strindberg (note, 431).

5. Ibid., 44, 50.

6. Gary Snyder, *The Practice of the Wild* (San Francisco: North Point Press, 1990), 8.

7. Ibid., 9–11.

8. Ibid., 90.

9. W. S. Merwin, *Writings to an Unfinished Accompaniment* (New York: Atheneum, 1973), 112; *The Carrier of Ladders* (New York: Atheneum, 1970), 32; *The Compass Flower* (New York: Atheneum, 1977), 49. Merwin was awarded the Pulitzer Prize for *The Carrier of Ladders*.

10. W. S. Merwin, *Houses and Travellers* (New York: Atheneum: 1977), 22.

11. Ibid.

12. John Keats, *The Poems of John Keats*, ed. Jack Stillinger (Cambridge, Mass.: Belknap Press, 1978), 104.

13. W. S. Merwin, *The Lice* (New York: Atheneum, 1967), 80.

14. Merwin, *Houses and Travellers*, 22.

15. Ibid., 23.

16. Henry David Thoreau, *Walden* (1854; reprint, New York: NAL, 1960), 66.

17. William Rueckert, "Literature and Ecology: An Experiment in Ecocriticism," in *The Ecocriticism Reader: Landmarks in Literary Ecology*, ed. Cheryll Glotfelty and Harold Fromm (Athens, Ga.: University of Georgia Press, 1996), 111.

18. Ibid., 110, 120.

19. Merwin, *The Compass Flower*, 43.

20. Ibid.

21. Ibid.

22. Ibid.

23. Keats, 103.

24. Merwin, *The Compass Flower*, 16.

25. Ibid., 15.

26. Glen A. Love, *The Ecocriticism Reader*, 235.

27. Ed Folsom, "'I Have Been a Long Time in a Strange Country': W. S. Merwin and America," in *W. S. Merwin: Essays on the Poetry*, ed. Cary Nelson and Ed Folsom (Urbana: University of Illinois Press, 1987), 232.

28. Ibid.

29. W. S. Merwin, "'Fact Has Two Faces': Interview," interview by Ed Folsom and Cary Nelson, in *Regions of Memory: Uncollected Prose, 1949–82*, ed. Ed Folsom and Cary Nelson (Urbana: University of Illinois Press, 1987), 323–24.

30. Thoreau, *Walden*, 70.

31. W. S. Merwin, *Opening The Hand* (New York: Atheneum, 1983), 80.

32. Merwin, *The Compass Flower*, 44.

33. Ibid.

34. Ibid.

35. Merwin, *Opening the Hand*, 80.

36. Charles Altieri, *Enlarging the Temple: New Directions in American Poetry during the 1960s* (Lewisburg, Pa.: Bucknell University Press, 1979), 199.

37. The quote is taken from Merwin's introduction to *Transparence of the World*, his translation of the poems of Jean Follain, (New York: Atheneum, 1969), vi–vii. The quotation Altieri refers to is from an introduction to poems of Jean Follain, which Merwin published in *The Atlantic Monthly* in 1969. The material I have quoted is essentially the same as that which appeared in *The Atlantic Monthly*.

38. Ibid., vi.

39. Merwin, *Opening the Hand*, 63.

40. Ibid.

41. Merwin, *Writings to an Unfinished Accompaniment*, 56.

42. Ibid.

43. Ibid.

44. Mark Christhilf, *W. S. Merwin the Mythmaker* (Columbia: University of Missouri Press, 1986), 47–48.

45. Merwin, *Houses and Travellers*, 206.

46. Ibid.

47. Thoreau, *Walden*, 109–10. Despite Thoreau's praise in this passage for Native American culture, he is not always consistently understanding of the Indian. When Joe Polis, his Penobscot Indian guide in *The Maine Woods*, attempts to tell him a local story of a mythical moose that turned into a mountain, he dismisses the tale as full of useless detail, and he dismisses Polis for speaking with a mystifying tone.

48. Ibid., 114.

49. Snyder, 80.

50. W. S. Merwin, *Selected Translations: 1968–1978* (New York: Atheneum, 1979), 77–78.

51. Ibid., 77.

52. Merwin, *Opening the Hand*, 83.

53. Ibid.

54. Ibid.

55. Ibid.

56. Ibid.

57. Keats, 89.

58. W. S. Merwin, *The Moving Target* (New York: Atheneum, 1963). 6.

59. Ibid., 6–7.

60. Ibid., 8.

61. Ibid., 7.

62. Ibid., 8.

63. Christhilf, 57–58.

64. Åke Hultkrantz, *The Religions of the American Indians*, trans. Monica Setterwall (Berkeley: University of California Press, 1979), 71–73.

65. Ibid., 71–72.

66. Merwin, *The Carrier of Ladders*, 119. Perdita's name, no doubt, is intended to bring to mind Shakespeare's character from *The Winter's Tale*, who also acts as an emblem of the natural because she was found as a baby abandoned to the waves, in adulthood serves as queen of the feast, and is pronounced by Florizel to be Flora herself.

67. Ibid., 120.

68. Ibid.

69. W. S. Merwin, *The Vixen* (New York: Knopf, 1996), 69.

70. Ibid.

71. Ibid.

72. Hultkrantz, 67–69.

73. Merwin, *The Carrier of Ladders*, 15.

74. Ibid., 16.

75. Ibid., 18.

76. Ibid., 19.

77. Ibid.

78. Ibid.

Chapter 2. Division

1. Hayden White, "The Forms of Wildness," in *The Wild Man Within: An Image in Western Thought from the Renaissance to Romanticism*, ed. Edward Dudley and Maximillian Novak (Pittsburgh, Pa.: University of Pittsburgh Press, 1972) 28.

2. Merwin, *The Carrier of Ladders*, 123.

3. Ibid.

4. Ibid.

5. Merwin, *Writings to an Unfinished Accompaniment*, 27.

6. Ibid.

7. Thoreau, 23–24.

8. W. S. Merwin. *The Rain in the Trees* (New York: Knopf, 1988), 72–73.

9. Merwin, *Writings to an Unfinished Accompaniment*, 27.

10. W. S. Merwin, "Where the Soul Lives," *The Power of the Word*, ed. Bill Moyers (Public Affairs Television, 20 October 1989), 17.

11. A. R. Ammons, *Garbage* (New York: Norton, 1993), 85.

12. Ibid.

13. W. S. Merwin, "W. S. Merwin," interview by Daniel Bourne, *Artful Dodge*, no. 3 (fall 1982): 15.

14. Merwin, *Writings to an Unfinished Accompaniment*, 15.

15. Ibid.

16. Ibid., 24.

17. Ibid., 15.

18. Ibid., 24.

19. Ibid., 24.

20. Walt Whitman, *Leaves of Grass*, ed. Malcolm Cowley (1855; reprint, Harmondsworth, England, 1976), 46.

21. Ibid., 45.

22. Thomas B. Byers, *What I Cannot Say: Self, Word, and World in Whitman, Stevens, and Merwin* (Urbana: University of Illinois Press, 1989), 112.

23. Merwin, *The Carrier of Ladders*, 66.

24. Ibid.

25. Ibid.

26. Ibid.

27. Ibid., 3; *Writings to an Unfinished Accompaniment*, 24.

28. Merwin, *The Carrier of Ladders*, 3.

29. Ibid.

30. Wendell Berry, *The Unsettling of America: Culture and Agriculture* (San Francisco: Sierra Club Books, 1977), 56.

31. Ibid.

32. Ibid. Notably, "Bread" is dedicated to Wendell Berry.

33. Ibid.

34. J. Hector St. John de Crèvecoeur, *Letters from an American Farmer*, in *Letters from an American Farmer and Sketches of Eighteenth-Century America* (1782; reprint, New York: Penguin Classics, 1986), 71.

35. Merwin, *Writings to an Unfinished Accompaniment*, 46.

36. Henry David Thoreau, *The Maine Woods*, in *Henry David Thoreau*, ed. Robert F. Sayre, *Library of America*, vol. 28 (New York: Literary Classics of the United States, 1985), 622.

37. Merwin, *The Rain in the Trees*, 55.

38. Ibid.

39. Ibid.

40. W. S. Merwin, "Where the Soul Lives," 17.

41. Merwin, *The Rain in the Trees*, 11.

42. Ibid.

43. Snyder, 37. 40.

44. Ibid., 41.

45. Ibid., 43.

46. Merwin, *The Rain in the Trees*, 11–12.

Chapter 3. The Disembodied Narrator

1. Charles Molesworth, "W. S. Merwin: Style, Vision, Influence," in *W. S. Merwin: Essays on the Poetry*, ed. Cary Nelson and Ed Folsom (Urbana: University of Illinois Press, 1987), 152.

2. Ibid., 148.

3. Merwin, *The Carrier of Ladders*, 38. Merwin probably has in mind the skylark, immortalized in Shelley's "To a Skylark." The skylark, an Old World lark that is found commonly in Europe and that travels into Asia and northern Africa, voices its melodious song when descending, after having flown upward almost vertically; Herbert G. Diegnan, "Skylark," in *Collier's Encyclopedia*, 1993 ed. Merwin's lark delivers its song as it falls from the sky.

4. Neal Bowers, "W. S. Merwin and Postmodern American Poetry," *Sewanee Review* 98 (1990): 249.

5. Merwin, *The Compass Flower*, 10.

6. Ibid.

7. Ibid.

8. Ibid.

9. Merwin, *The Carrier of Ladders*, 75.

10. Ibid.

11. Ibid.

12. Laurence Lieberman, "New Poetry: The Church of Ash," review of *Writings to an Unfinished Accompaniment*, by W. S. Merwin, *Yale Review* 62 (June 1973): 603.

13. Joseph Campbell, *The Flight of the Wild Gander: Explorations in the Mythological Dimension* (New York: Viking Press, 1969; New York: HarperPerennial, 1990), 197–98.

14. Merwin, *The Moving Target*, 50.

15. Merwin, *Writings to an Unfinished Accompaniment*, 95.

16. Ibid. See Matthew 9:20 and 14:36.

17. Ibid.

18. Jarold Ramsey, "The Continuities of W. S. Merwin: 'What Has Escaped Us, We Bring with Us,'" in *W. S. Merwin: Essays on the Poetry* (Urbana: University of Illinois Press, 1987), 36–37.

19. Ibid.

20. Willis G. Regier, introduction to *Masterpieces of American Indian Literature* (New York: MJF Books, 1993), xi; Charles Alexander Eastman (Ohiyesa), *The Soul of the Indian*, 1911; reprinted in *Masterpieces of American Indian Literature*, 154.

21. Eastman, 155.

22. Merwin, *The Carrier of Ladders*, 54.

23. Ibid.

24. Merwin, *The Rain in the Trees*, 75.

25. Aldo Leopold, *A Sand County Almanac: With Essays on Conservation from Round River* (Oxford: Oxford University Press, 1949, 1953; reprint, New York: Ballantine, 1966), 253.

CHAPTER 4. SILENCE

1. Richard Howard, *Alone with America: Essays on the Art of Poetry in the United States since 1950*, enl. ed. (New York: Atheneum, 1980), 432, 428.

2. W. S. Merwin, "Possibilities of the Unknown: Conversations with W. S. Merwin," interview by Jack Myers and Michael Simms, *Southwest Review*, no. 2 (spring 1983): 168.

3. Ibid., 168–69.

4. Ibid., 169.

5. Cary Nelson, "The Resources of Failure: W. S. Merwin's Deconstructive Career," in *W. S. Merwin: Essays on the Poetry*, ed. Cary Nelson and Ed Folsom (Urbana: University of Illinois Press, 1987), 114.

6. Byers, 108.

7. Gerald L. Bruns, *Modern Poetry and the Idea of Language: A Critical and Historical Study* (New Haven: Yale University Press, 1974), 190.

8. Ibid., 205.

9. Merwin, *The Carrier of Ladders*, 37.

10. Ibid.

11. W. S. Merwin, "An Interview with W. S. Merwin," interview by David L. Elliott, *Contemporary Literature*, no. 1 (spring 1988): 5.

12. W. S. Merwin, "Aspects of a Mountain," in *Regions of Memory: Uncollected Prose, 1949–82*, ed. Ed Folsom and Cary Nelson (Urbana: University of Illinois Press, 1987), 137–38.

13. Merwin, *Writings to an Unfinished Accompaniment*, 55.

14. Ibid.

15. Lieberman, 613.

16. Michel Foucault, *The Order of Things: An Archaeology of the Human Sciences*, translation of *Les Mots et les choses* (New York: Vintage, 1973), 59.

17. Merwin, *The Moving Target*, 40.

18. Merwin, *The Lice*, 24.

19. Ibid., 45.

20. Merwin, *The Moving Target*, 97.

21. W. S. Merwin's writings that specifically deal with his years in southwest France are, most importantly, his 1992 book of stories, *The Lost Upland*, and his 1996 volume of poetry, *The Vixen*. Both focus on village life in the region and the people of the villages. In France, Merwin appears to have found a community of persons he admired and, among them, a basically justifiable relationship to the environment. In both books, we find Merwin's most descriptive and often charming portraits of people.

22. Merwin, *The Carrier of Ladders*, 138.

23. Ibid., 116–17.

24. Ibid., 28–29.

25. David Pollard, *The Poetry of Keats: Language and Experience* (Sussex: Harvester Press, 1984), 54–60.

26. Merwin, *Writings to an Unfinished Accompaniment*, 91.

27. Ibid.

28. Ibid.

29. James Wright, *The Branch Will Not Break* (Middletown, Conn.: Wesleyan University Press, 1963), 39.

30. Ibid.

31. Robert Bly, *Selected Poems*, (New York: Harper & Row, 1986), 29.

32. Ibid.

33. Ibid.

34. Ibid.

35. Merwin, *The Carrier of Ladders*, 114.

36. R. P. Blackmur, "The Language of Silence: A Citation," *Sewanee Review* 63 (1955): 382.

Chapter 5. Language and Nature

1. W. S. Merwin, "W. S. Merwin: An Interview," interview by Michael Pettit, *Black Warrior Review*, no. 2 (1982): 15.

2. Ibid., 16.

3. Robert Bly, "Where the Soul Lives," *The Power of the Word*, ed. Bill Moyers (Public Affairs Television, 20 October 1989), 11.

4. Merwin, "W. S. Merwin: An Interview," *Black Warrior Review*, 18. For an informative essay on the descriptive and conceptually unique languages of Native America, see Nancy Lord, "Native Tongues," *Sierra*, November/December 1996, 46–49, 68–69. Lord points out, for example, that the Dena'ina language of Alaska (once nearly extinct) offers single-word distinctions for "ridge broken up into knolls, almost bare," "ridge with knolls pointing up," "ridge sloping to a point," "pointed up mountain," and "sloping mountain" (47).

5. Merwin, *The Rain in The Trees*, 47.

6. Ibid.

7. Ibid.

8. Ibid.

9. Ibid., 67

10. Ibid.

11. Ibid.

12. Ibid.

13. Kenneth Burke, "The Vegetal Radicalism of Theodore Roethke," in *Modern Critical Views: Theodore Roethke,* ed. Harold Bloom (New York: Chelsea House, 1988), 17.

14. Rosemary Sullivan, "Wet with Another Life: 'Meditations of an Old Woman,'" in *Modern Critical Views: Theodore Roethke,* 146. The ouroboros used here is the image of the "snake that bites its own tail." In this usage, it is a Jungian symbol of an unconscious circular process that has no effect upon consciousness: C. G. Jung, *Letters,* ed. Gerhard Adler, trans. R. F. C. Hull, Bollingen Series 95, vol. 1 (Princeton, N.J.: Princeton University Press, 1973), 371.

15. Merwin, *The Rain in the Trees,* 60.

16. Ibid.

17. Ibid.

18. W. S. Merwin, "The Tree on One Tree Hill," *Mānoa* 3 (1991): 1, 7, 11–12.

19. Ibid., 12.

20. Ibid., 14.

21. Ibid., 12–13.

22. Ibid., 13.

23. Ibid., 14.

24. W. S. Merwin, *Travels* (New York: Knopf, 1993), 3.

25. Ibid., 4.

26. Merwin, *The Rain in the Trees,* 77.

27. Ibid., 50.

28. Ibid., 77.

29. Ibid., 50.

CHAPTER 6. NEW WORLD CONQUERORS AND THE ENVIRONMENTAL CRISIS

1. W. S. Merwin, "W. S. Merwin: An Interview," interview by Michael Clifton, *American Poetry Review,* no. 4 (July-August 1983): 17.

2. Ibid., 21.

3. Snyder, 131.

4. Snyder, 99–102.

5. Fergus M. Bordewich, *Killing the White Man's Indian: Reinventing Native Americans at the End of the Twentieth Century* (New York: Doubleday, 1996), 212.

6. Ibid.

7. Donald Worster, "The Vulnerable Earth: Toward a Planetary History," in *The Ends of the Earth: Perspectives on Modern Environmental History,* ed. Donald Worster (Cambridge: Cambridge University Press, 1988), 9–10.

8. Peter Matthiessen, *Indian Country* (New York: Viking, 1984), 9.

9. Roy Harvey Pearce, *Savagism and Civilization: A Study of the Indian and the American Mind* (Berkeley: University of California Press, 1988), 3.

10. Ibid., 41–49; 151–60.

11. Peter Nabokov, ed. *Native American Testimony: A Chronicle of Indian-White Relations from Prophecy to the Present, 1492–1992.* (New York: Viking, 1991), 70.

12. Frank N. Magill, "Powell, John Wesley," *Great Lives from History,* American Series, vol. 4 (Pasadena, Calif.: Salem Press, 1987), 1832–34.

13. Merwin, *The Carrier of Ladders,* 49.

14. Ibid.

15. Matthiessen, 10.

16. Folsom, 242.

17. Merwin, *The Carrier of Ladders*, 48.

18. Ibid.

19. Ibid.

20. Ibid., 50.

21. Carl Waldman, *Atlas of the North American Indian* (New York: Facts on File, 1985), 183–85.

22. Edward J. Brunner, *Poetry as Labor and Privilege: The Writings of W. S. Merwin* (Urbana: University of Illinois Press, 1991), 104–5; 305–6.

23. W. S. Merwin, "W. S. Merwin: An Interview," *American Poetry Review*, 22.

24. Merwin, *The Rain in the Trees*, 61. It is recorded that upon first seeing the large, masted ships of Captain James Cook, which appeared off the coast of Kauai in January 1778, one Hawaiian called them "trees moving about on the sea." The enormous sails also reminded them of the image of the hero-god Lono, which consisted of a long pole with a representation of the god's head atop it and a crosspiece from which hung two long sheets of white kapa, or cloth. Feather streamers, ferns, and the outer skin and feathers of sea birds also hung along the crosspiece. As the image was carried around the island during the makahiki season (a festival commemorating the gifts of Lono to the people), taxes were collected. The kapa cloth of the image resembled the cloud signs and storms with which Lono is associated. In "The Strangers from the Horizon," Merwin simply has the Hawaiians refer to the sails as "clouds," but by this description Lono is automatically evoked in the Hawaiian's mind. Hawaiian canoes often had sails; however, they were, of course, much smaller.

On Cook's subsequent visit to Hawaii, his ships harbored at Kealakekua Bay, sacred to Lono, on January 16, 1779. Again arriving during the makahiki festival, Cook was initially revered as the returning god Lono and his sailors as companion-gods. Within a very short period of time, the natives realized by their appetites for women and food that the mariners were not gods. In early trading with Cook's men, Hawaiians were offered only one English nail for two pigs. During a controversy over possession of the ship's cutter, Cook was killed on February 14, 1779, by the warriors of King Kalaniopuu, some wielding English iron weapons. For more information about and images from the history of Hawaii, see Joseph Feher, compiler, *Hawaii: A Pictorial History*, text by Edward Joesting and O. A. Bushnell (Honolulu: Bishop Museum Press, 1969), 52–54, 111, 134–38.

25. Ibid., 61.

26. Feher, 134–38.

27. Ibid., 62

28. Ibid.

29. Michael Kioni Dudley, *A Hawaiian Nation I: Man, Gods, and Nature* (Honolulu: Nā Kāne O Ka Malo Press, 1990), 81–82.

30. Ibid., 48.

31. Martha Beckwith, *Hawaiian Mythology* (Yale University Press, 1940; Honolulu: University of Hawaii Press, 1970), 60–62.

32. Ibid., 60; Dudley, 82.

33. Merwin, *The Rain in the Trees*, 71.

34. Ibid.

35. Ibid.

36. Ibid.

37. Dudley, 50.

38. Merwin, *The Rain in the Trees*, 69.

39. W. S. Merwin, "The Sacred Bones of Maui," *New York Times Magazine*, 6 August 1989, 21, 34–35.

40. Merwin, *The Rain in the Trees*, 63.
41. Ibid.
42. Merwin, *Opening the Hand*, 43.
43. Merwin, "An Interview with W. S. Merwin," 23.
44. Ibid., 24.
45. Although in this poem the cinchona plants of Richard Spruce die when transplanted to India, cinchona was successfully cultivated in India, Java, and Malaya in the mid-nineteenth century. Cinchona had been introduced to Europe 200 years earlier after the Condesa Chinchon, wife of the Spanish governor of Peru, had been cured of malaria in 1638 by use of its bark. Demand for quinine and reckless methods of harvesting the bark once threatened the indigenous plants with extinction; John A. Borneman, Jr., "Cinchona," in *Collier's Encyclopedia*, 1993 ed.
46. Merwin, "An Interview with W. S. Merwin," 7.

Chapter 7. The Vanishing Planet

1. Merwin, *The Lice*, 68.
2. Ibid., 68–69.
3. Merwin, "'Fact Has Two Faces': Interview," 329–30.
4. Merwin, *The Lice*, 41.
5. Ibid., 3.
6. Maxine Kumin, *Nurture* (New York: Penguin, 1989), 10.
7. Ibid.
8. Ibid., 19.
9. Ibid.
10. W. S. Merwin, "On the Bestial Floor," *The Nation*, 22 March 1965, 313.
11. Donald Worster, *Nature's Economy: A History of Ecological Ideas*, 2d ed. (Cambridge: Cambridge University Press, 1994), 66.
12. Merwin, *The Lice*, 73.
13. Ibid.
14. Ibid., 72.
15. W. S. Merwin, "Letter from Aldermaston," *The Nation*, 7 May 1960, 408–10; "Act of Conscience," *The Nation*, 29 December 1962, 463–80; "The Terrible Meek, *The Nation*, 16 June 1962, 533–36; "A New Right Arm," in *Regions of Memory: Uncollected Prose, 1949–82*, 253–66.
16. Merwin, "W. S. Merwin: An Interview," interview by Michael Clifton, 22.
17. Merwin, "Possibilities of the Unknown: Conversations with W. S. Merwin," 171.
18. Merwin, *Opening the Hand*, 33.
19. Ibid.
20. Merwin, *The Rain in the Trees*, 30.
21. Merwin, *Opening the Hand*, 33.
22. Ibid.
23. "Shaving Without a Mirror" is not one of Merwin's better poems, yet I have included it for its portrayal of the concepts I have discussed. Despite the fact that *Opening the Hand* (1983) and *The Compass Flower* (1977) contain many excellent poems, several critics have remarked that the volumes are not as strong as others. I must agree that these two volumes and Merwin's experiment with haikulike verse, *Finding the Islands* (1982), are not as consistently powerful as other volumes beginning with *The Moving Target* (1963), in which he moved to the broken lines and stanzas of his "deep image" verse.
24. Merwin, *The Rain in the Trees*, 30.

25. Merwin, *The Moving Target*, 94.

26. W. S. Merwin, *The Miner's Pale Children* (New York: Atheneum, 1970), 85–86.

27. Ibid., 85.

28. Ibid., 88.

29. Ibid.

30. Ibid.

31. Merwin, *The Compass Flower*, 71.

32. W. S. Merwin, *W. S. Merwin*, interview by Joseph Parisi and James Richardson, audiotape, 1991, Modern Poetry Association, Chicago.

33. Merwin, *The Rain in the Trees*, 41.

34. Ibid.

35. Ibid.

36. Ibid.

37. Ibid., 51.

38. Merwin, *The Lice*, 75.

39. Ibid., 68.

40. W. S. Merwin, *W. S. Merwin*, interview by Lewis MacAdams, videocassete, 1989, Lannan Literary Foundation, Los Angeles.

41. W. S. Merwin, *The Rain in the Trees*, 46.

42. Ibid.

43. Ibid., 49.

44. Ibid.

45. Snyder, 37.

46. Merwin, "W. S. Merwin: An Interview," interview by Michael Clifton, 21; Merwin, "An Interview with W. S. Merwin," interview by David. L. Elliott, 23–24; W. S. Merwin, "Letter on the Wao Kele O Puna Rain Forest," *American Poetry Review* 19, no. 2 (1990): 43–45.

47. Merwin, "Letter on the Wao Kele O Puna Rain Forest," 43.

48. Ibid.

49. Merwin, *The Rain in the Trees*, 66.

50. Ibid.

51. Ibid.

52. Ibid., 26.

53. Ibid.

54. Ibid.

55. Merwin, "W. S. Merwin: An Interview," interview by Michael Clifton, 22.

56. John Elder, *Imagining the Earth: Poetry and the Vision of Nature* (Urbana: University of Illinois Press, 1985), 57.

57. Merwin, *The Vixen*, 17.

Works Cited

PRIMARY WORKS

POETRY

The Carrier of Ladders. New York: Atheneum, 1970.
The Compass Flower. New York: Atheneum, 1977.
The Lice. New York: Atheneum, 1967,
The Moving Target. New York: Atheneum, 1963.
Opening the Hand. New York: Atheneum, 1983.
The Rain in the Trees. New York: Knopf, 1988.
Travels. New York: Knopf, 1993.
The Vixen. New York: Knopf, 1996.
Writings to an Unfinished Accompaniment. New York: Atheneum, 1973.

PROSE

Houses and Travellers. New York: Atheneum, 1977.
The Miner's Pale Children. New York: Atheneum, 1970.

ARTICLES

"Act of Conscience." *The Nation*, 29 December 1962, 463–80.
"Aspects of a Mountain." In *Regions of Memory: Uncollected Prose, 1949-82*, ed. Ed Folsom
  and Cary Nelson. Urbana: University of Illinois Press, 1987.
"Letter from Aldermaston." *The Nation*, 7 May 1960, 408–10.
"Letter on the Wao Kele O Puna Rain Forest." *American Poetry Review* 19 (March-April
  1990): 43–45.
"A New Right Arm." In *Regions of Memory: Uncollected Prose, 1949–82*, ed. Ed Folsom
  and Cary Nelson. Urbana: University of Illinois Press, 1987: 253–66.
"On the Bestial Floor." *The Nation*, 22 March 1965: 313–14.
"The Sacred Bones of Maui." *New York Times Magazine*, 6 August 1989, 20–21, 34–35.

"The Terrible Meek." *The Nation*, 16 June 1962: 533–36.
"The Tree on One Tree Hill." *Mānoa* 3, no.1 (1991): 1–19.

TRANSLATIONS

Selected Translations: 1968–1978. New York: Atheneum, 1979.
Foreword. *Transparence of the World*, by Jean Follain. New York: Atheneum, 1969.

SECONDARY WORKS

CRITICAL BOOKS

Altieri, Charles. *Enlarging the Temple: New Directions in American Poetry during the 1960s*. Lewisburg, Pa: Bucknell University Press, 1979.

Brunner, Edward. J. *Poetry as Labor and Privelege: The Writings of W. S. Merwin*. Urbana, IL: University of Illinois Press, 1991.

Byers, Thomas B. *What I Cannot Say: Self, Word, and World in Whitman, Stevens and Merwin*. Urbana, IL: University of Illinois Press, 1989.

Christhilf, Mark. *W. S. Merwin, the Mythmaker*. Columbia: University of Missouri Press, 1986.

Howard, Richard. "W. S. Merwin." *Alone with America: Essays on the Art of Poetry in the United States since 1950*. Enlarged edition. New York: Atheneum, 1980.

ARTICLES

Bowers, Neal. "W. S. Merwin and Postmodern American Poetry." *Sewanee Review* 98, no. 2 (1990): 246–59.

Folsom, Ed. "'I Have Been a Long Time in a Strange Country': W. S. Merwin and America." In *W. S. Merwin: Essays on the Poetry*, ed. Cary Nelson and Ed Folsom, 224–49. Urbana: University of Illinois Press, 1987.

Hirsch, Edward. Introduction to "The Art of Poetry XXXVIII: W. S. Merwin." *Paris Review* 29, no. 102 (1987): 57–81.

Maranto, Gina. "A Tender of Trees: W. S. Merwin's Poetry and Politics." *Amicus Journal* 14, no. 1 (1992): 12–14.

Molesworth, Charles. "W. S. Merwin: Style, Vision, Influence." In *W. S. Merwin: Essays on the Poetry*, ed. Cary Nelson and Ed Folsom, 145–58. Urbana: University of Illinois Press, 1987.

Nelson, Cary. "The Resources of Failure: W. S. Merwin's Deconstructive Career." In *W. S. Merwin: Essays on the Poetry*, ed. Cary Nelson and Ed Folsom, 78–121. Urbana: University of Illinois Press, 1987.

Ramsey, Jarold. "The Continuities of W. S. Merwin: 'What Has Escaped Us, We Bring with Us.'" In *W. S. Merwin, Essays on the Poetry*, ed. Cary Nelson and Ed Folsom, 19–44. Urbana: University of Illinois Press, 1987.

REVIEW

Lieberman, Laurence. "New Poetry: The Church of Ash." Review of *Writings to an Unfinished Accompaniment*, by W. S. Merwin. *Yale Review* 62 (1973): 602–13.

INTERVIEWS AND RECORDINGS:

"W. S. Merwin." Interview by Daniel Bourne, *Artful Dodge*, no. 3 (fall 1982): 9–17.

"W. S. Merwin: An Interview." Interview by Michael Clifton. *American Poetry Review*, no. 4 (July-August 1983): 17–22.

"An Interview with W. S. Merwin." Interview by David L. Elliott, *Contemporary Literature*, no. 1 (spring 1988): 1–25.

"'Fact Has Two Faces': Interview." Interview by Ed Folsom and Cary Nelson, In *Regions of Memory: Uncollected Prose, 1949–82*, ed. Ed Folsom and Cary Nelson. Urbana: University of Illinois Press, 1987.

W. S. Merwin. Interview by Lewis MacAdams. Lannan Literary Foundation, 1989. Videocassette.

"Where the Soul Lives." Interview by Bill Moyers, *The Power of the Word*, Public Affairs Television, 20 October 1989.

"Possibilities of the Unknown: Conversations with W. S. Merwin." Interview by Jack Myers and Michael Simms, *Southwest Review*, no. 2 (spring 1983): 164–80.

W. S. Merwin. Interview by Joseph Parisi and James Richardson. Modern Poetry Association, 1991. Audiotape.

"W. S. Merwin: An Interview." Interview by Michael Pettit, *Black Warrior Review*, no. 2 (spring 1982): 7–20.

ADDITIONAL SOURCES

Ammons, A. R. *Garbage*. New York: Norton, 1993.

Beckwith, Martha. *Hawaiian Mythology*. Yale University Press, 1940. Reprint, Honolulu: University of Hawaii Press, 1970.

Berry, Wendell. *The Unsettling of America: Culture and Agriculture*. San Francisco: Sierra Club Books, 1977.

Blackmur, R. P. "The Language of Silence: A Citation." *Sewanee Review* 63 (July-September 1955): 382–404.

Bly, Robert. *Selected Poems*. New York: Harper & Row, 1986.

Bordewich, Fergus M. *Killing the White Man's Indian: Reinventing Native Americans at the End of the Twentieth Century*. New York: Doubleday, 1996.

Bruns, Gerald L. *Modern Poetry and the Idea of Language: A Critical and Historical Study*. New Haven, Conn.: Yale University Press, 1974.

Buell, Lawrence. *The Environmental Imagination: Thoreau, Nature Writing, and the Formation of American Culture*. Cambridge, Mass.: Belknap Press, 1995.

Burke, Kenneth. "The Vegetal Radicalism of Theodore Roethke." In *Modern Critical Views: Theodore Roethke*, ed. Harold Bloom. New York: Chelsea House, 1988, 7–36.

Campbell, Joseph. *The Flight of the Wild Gander: Explorations in the Mythological Dimensions.* New York: Viking Press, 1969. Reprint, New York: HarperPerennial, 1990.

Dudley, Michael Kioni. *A Hawaiian Nation I: Man, Gods, and Nature.* Honolulu: Nā Kāne O Ka Malo Press, 1990.

Eastman, Charles Alexander (Ohiyesa). *The Soul of the Indian.* 1911. Reprinted in *Masterpieces of American Indian Literature*, ed. Willis G. Regier. New York: MJF Books, 1993, 143–91.

Elder, John. *Imagining the Earth: Poetry and the Vision of Nature.* Urbana: University of Illinois Press, 1985.

Feher, Joseph, compiler. *Hawaii: A Pictorial History.* Text by Edward Joesting and O. A. Bushnell. Honolulu: Bishop Museum Press, 1969.

Foucault, Michel. *The Order of Things: An Archaeology of the Human Sciences:* A translation of *Les Mots et les choses.* 1971. New York: Vintage, 1973.

Hultkrantz, Åke. *The Religions of the American Indians.* Translated by Monica Setterwall. Berkeley: University of California Press, 1979.

Jung, C. G. *Letters.* Edited by Gerhard Adler. Translated by R. F. C. Hull. Vol. 1. Bollingen Series, no. 95 Princeton: Princeton, N.J.: University Press, 1973.

Keats, John. *The Poems of John Keats.* Edited by Jack Stillinger. Cambridge, Mass.: Belknap Press, 1978.

Kumin, Maxine. *Nurture.* New York: Penguin, 1989.

Leopold, Aldo. *A Sand County Almanac.* In *A Sand County Almanac: With Essays on Conservation from Round River.* Oxford University Press, 1949. Reprint, New York: Ballantine, 1970.

Love, Glen A. "Revaluing Nature: Toward an Ecological Criticism." In *The Ecocriticism Reader: Landmarks in Literary Ecology.* ed. Cheryll Glotfelty and Harold Fromm. Athens: University of Georgia Press, 1996, 225–40.

Matthiessen, Peter. *Indian Country.* New York: Viking, 1984.

Nabokov, Peter, ed. *Native American Testimony: A Chronicle of Indian-White Relations from Prophecy to the Present, 1492–1992.* New York: Viking, 1991.

Pearce, Roy Harvey. *Savagism and Civilization: A Study of the Indian and the American Mind.* Berkeley: University of California Press, 1988.

Pollard, David. *The Poetry of Keats: Language and Experience.* Sussex, England: Harvester Press, 1984.

"Powell, John Wesley." *Great Lives from History.* Pasadena, CA: Salem Press, American Series, 1987.

Regier, Willis G. Introduction to *Masterpieces of American Indian Literature.* New York: MJF Books, 1993.

Rueckert, William. "Literature and Ecology: An Experiment in Ecocriticism." In *The Ecocriticism Reader: Landmarks in Literary Ecology,* ed. Cheryll Glotfelty and Harold Fromm. Athens: University of Georgia Press, 1996, 105–23.

St. John de Crèvecoeur, J. Hector. *Letters from an American Farmer.* In *Letters from an American Farmer and Sketches of Eighteenth-Century America.* 1782. Reprint, New York: Penguin Classics, 1981.

Snyder, Gary. *The Practice of the Wild.* San Francisco: North Point Press, 1990.

Sullivan, Rosemary. "Wet with Another Life: 'Meditations of an Old Woman.'" In

Modern Critical Views: Theodore Roethke, ed. Harold Bloom. New York: Chelsea House, 1988, 141–58.

Thoreau, Henry David. *The Maine Woods*. In *Henry David Thoreau*. Edited by Robert F. Sayre. *Library of America*, vol. 28. New York: Literary Classics of the United States, 1985.

Thoreau, Henry David. *Walden*. 1854. Reprint, New York: NAL, 1960.

Waldman, Carl. *Atlas of the North American Indian*. New York: Facts on File Publications, 1985.

White, Hayden. "The Forms of Wildness." In *The Wild Man Within: An Image in Western Thought from the Renaissance to Romanticism*, ed. Edward Dudley and Maximillian Novak. Pittsburgh: University of Pittsburgh Press, 1972, 3–38.

Whitman, Walt. *Leaves of Grass*. Edited by Malcolm Cowley. 1855. Reprint, Harmondsworth, England: Penguin, 1976.

Worster, Donald. *Nature's Economy: A History of Ecological Ideas*, 2d ed. Cambridge: Cambridge University Press, 1994.

Worster, Donald. "The Vulnerable Earth: Toward a Planetary History." In *The Ends of the Earth: Perspectives on Modern Environmental History*, ed. Donald Worster. Cambridge: Cambridge University Press, 1988, 3–20.

Wright, James. *The Branch Will Not Break*. Middletown, Conn.: Wesleyan University Press, 1963.

Index